RAIMAZ Publishing
2019

First RAIMAZ Printing, June 2019
10 9 8 7 6 5 4 3 2 1

RAIMAZPublishing.com

ISBN 978-0-359-72050-7

VISUAL**MASTER**

VISUAL**MASTER** is a journal to help you sketch out your storyboard ideas on the go. Got the perfect scene running through your head? Start sketching it out. 50 sheets of 8 boards for you to rough out those amazing scenes [That's 400 boards!].

Collaborate with your friends and colleges and then finalize back at the office, or if you want use the journal to do your finals to present to clients, investors, etc.

It's your journal, do as you will... Speaking of this being your journal.

Journal Belongs to:

_____
Name

_____
Phone or EMAIL Address

If found, please contact the owner. :)

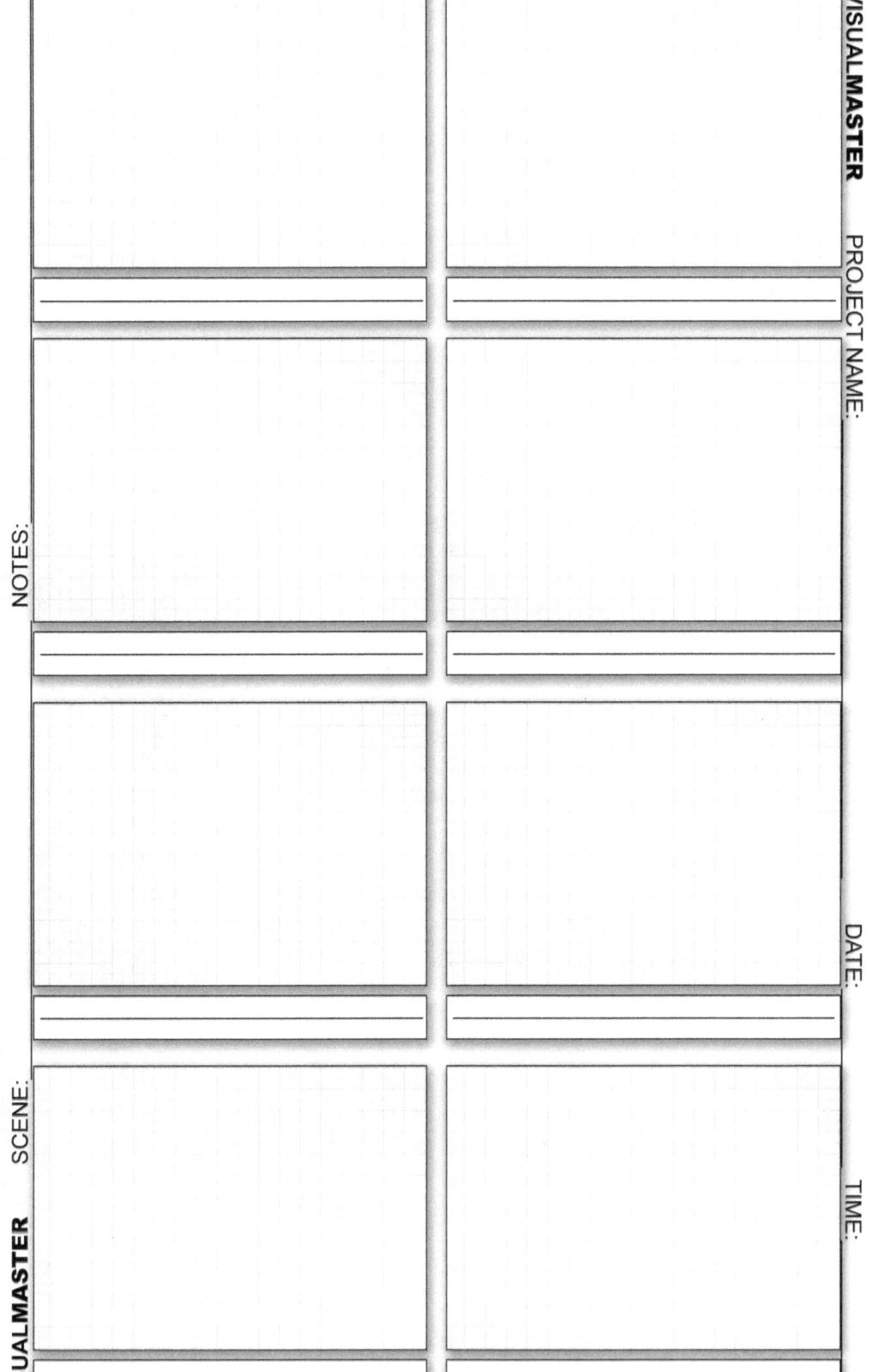

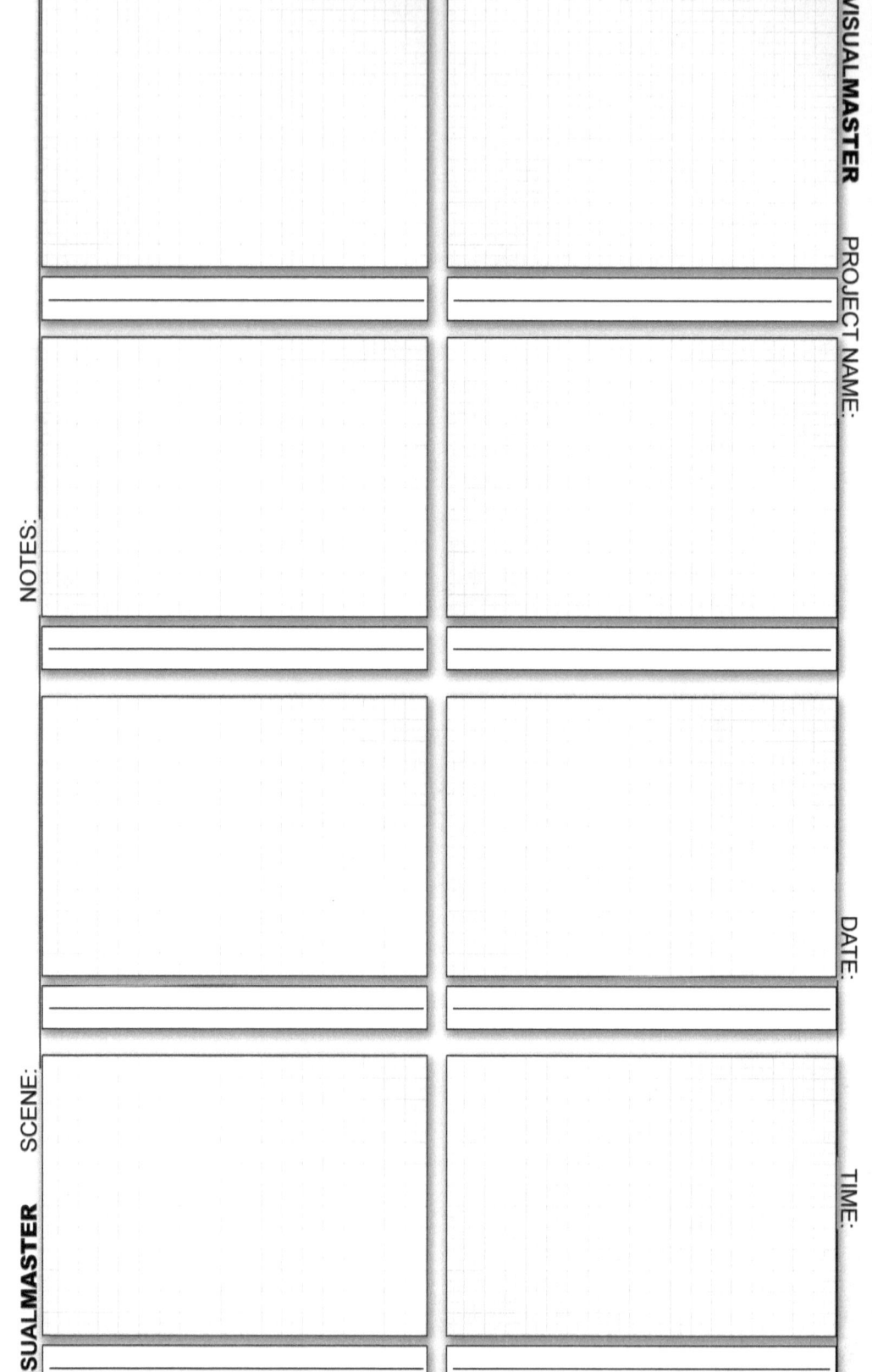

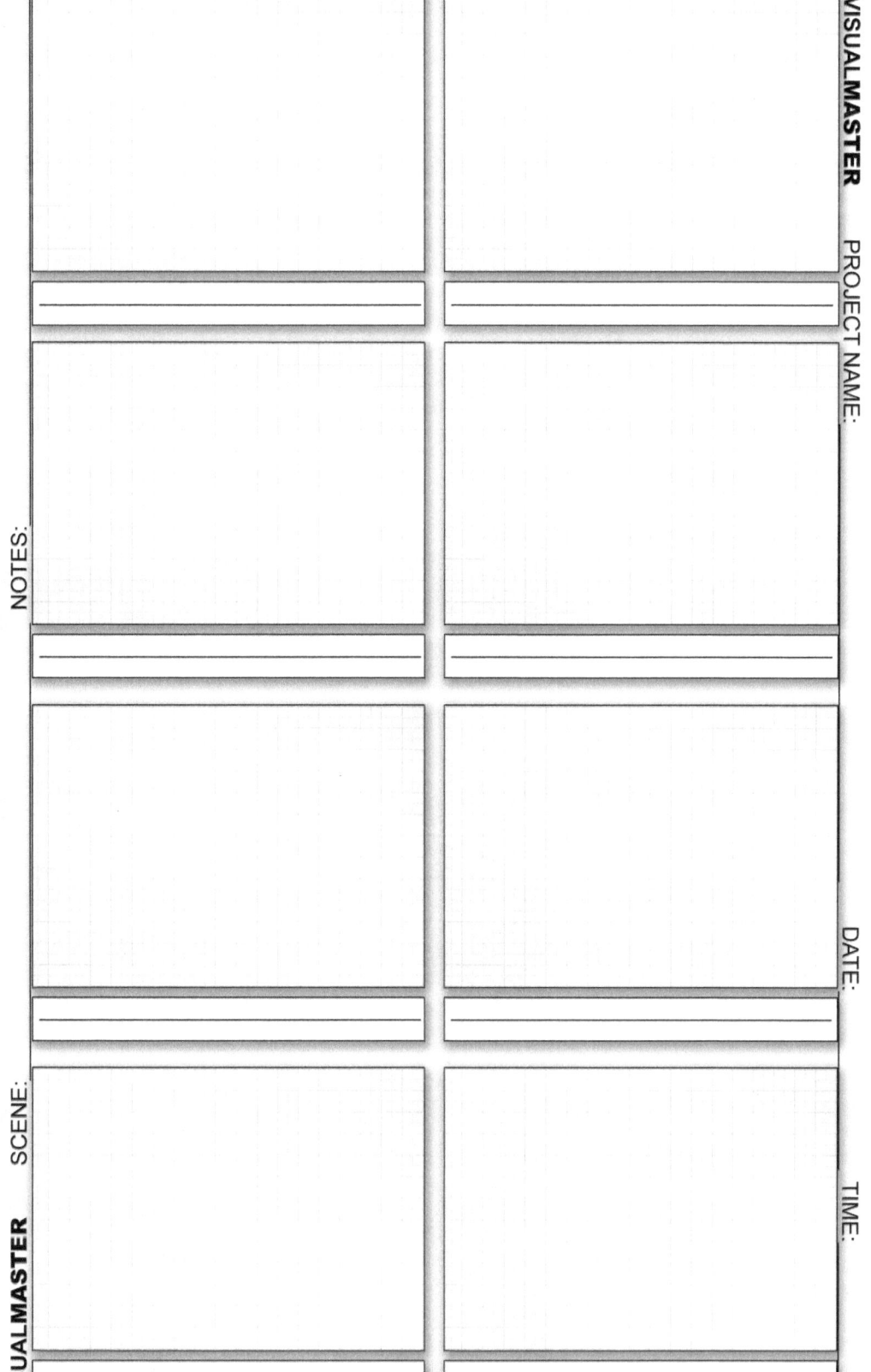

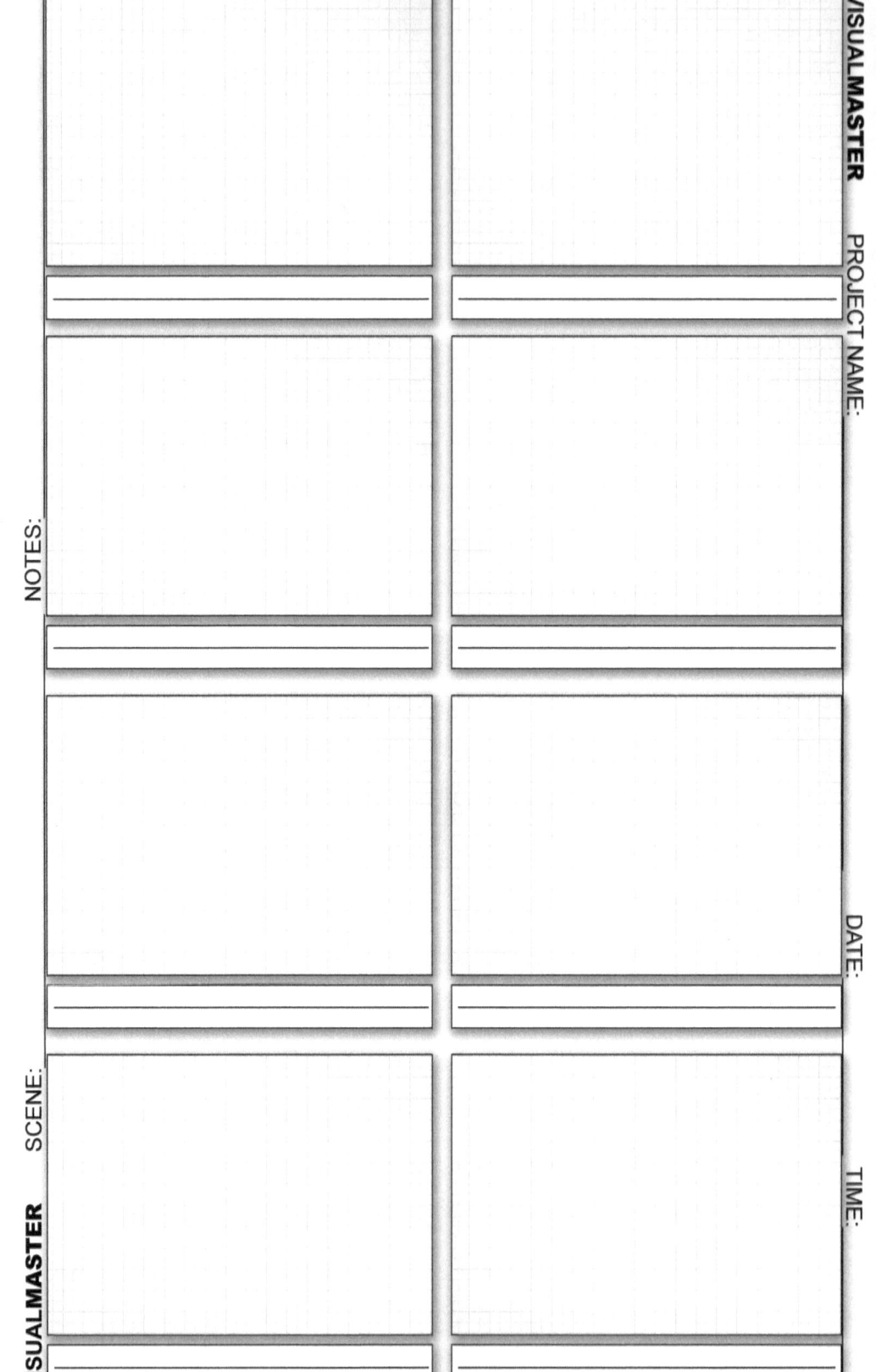

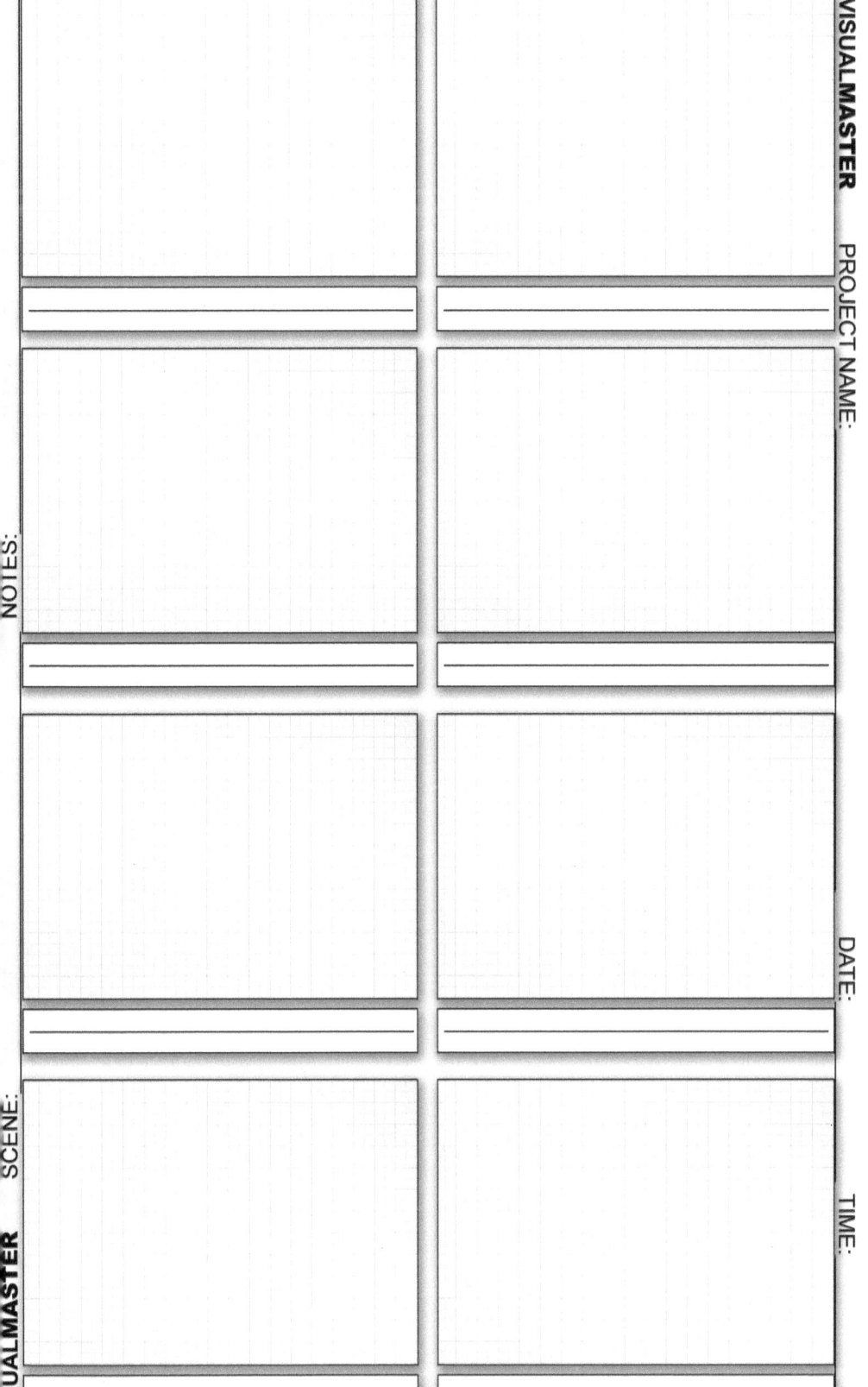

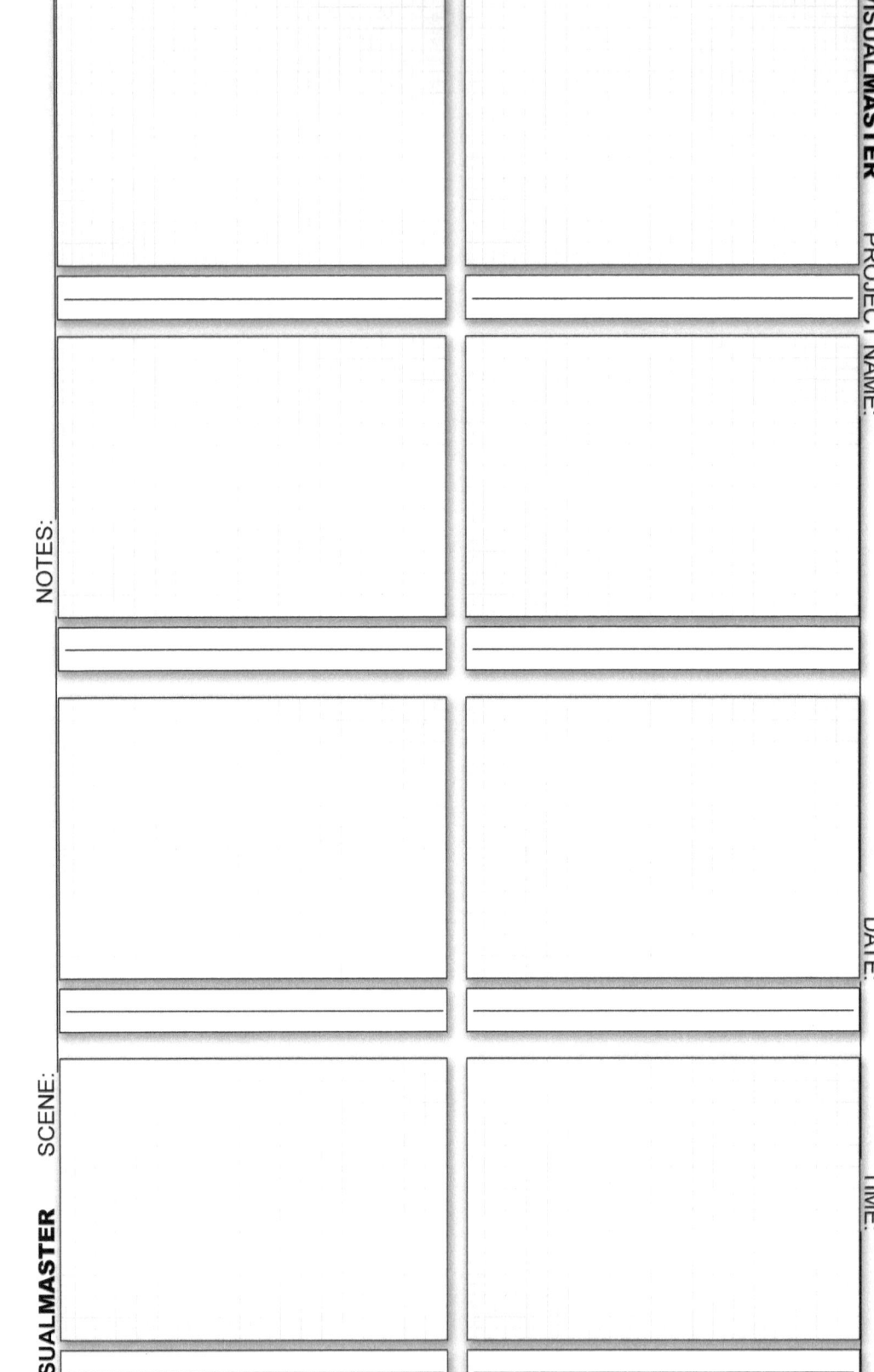

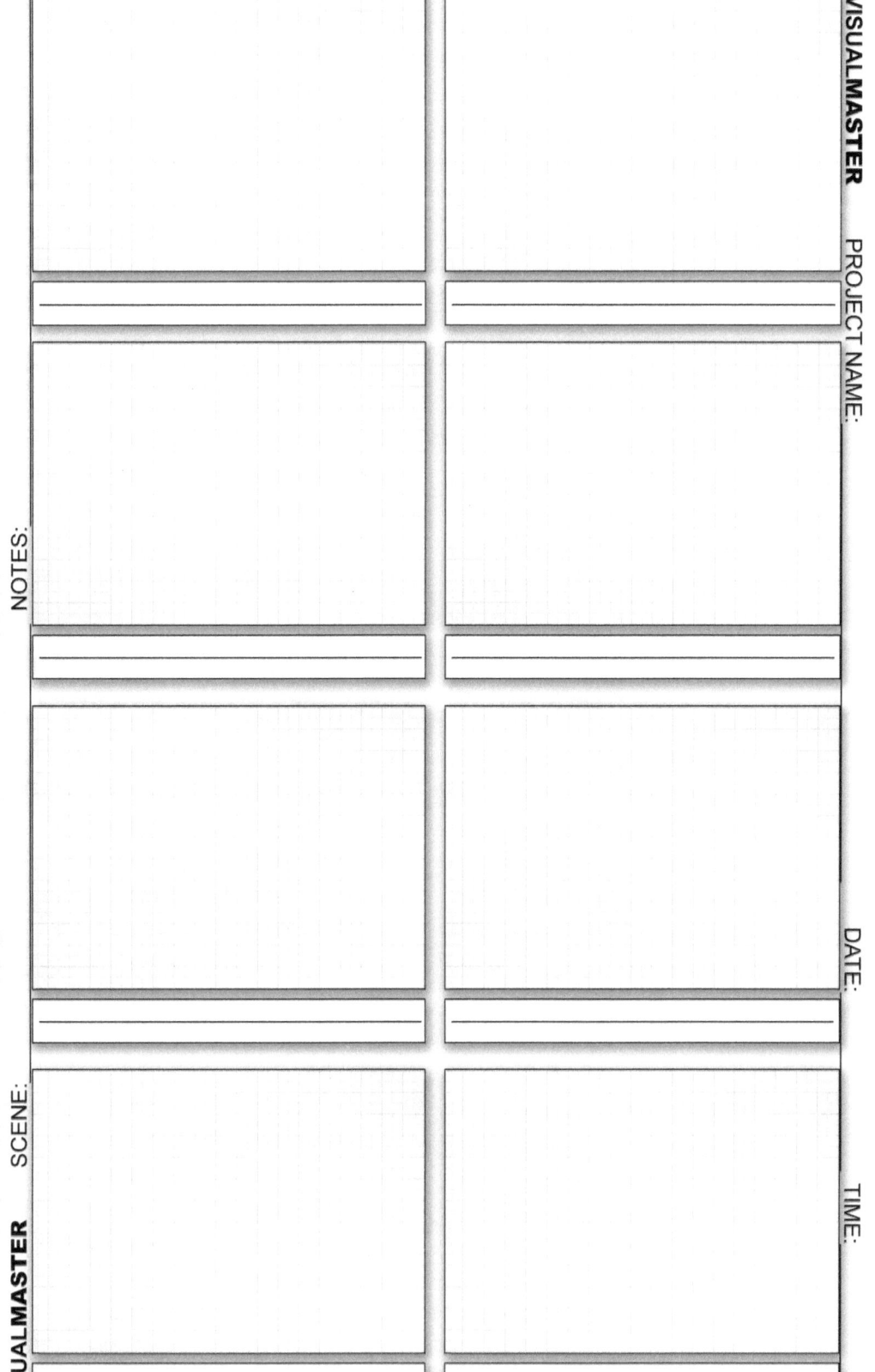

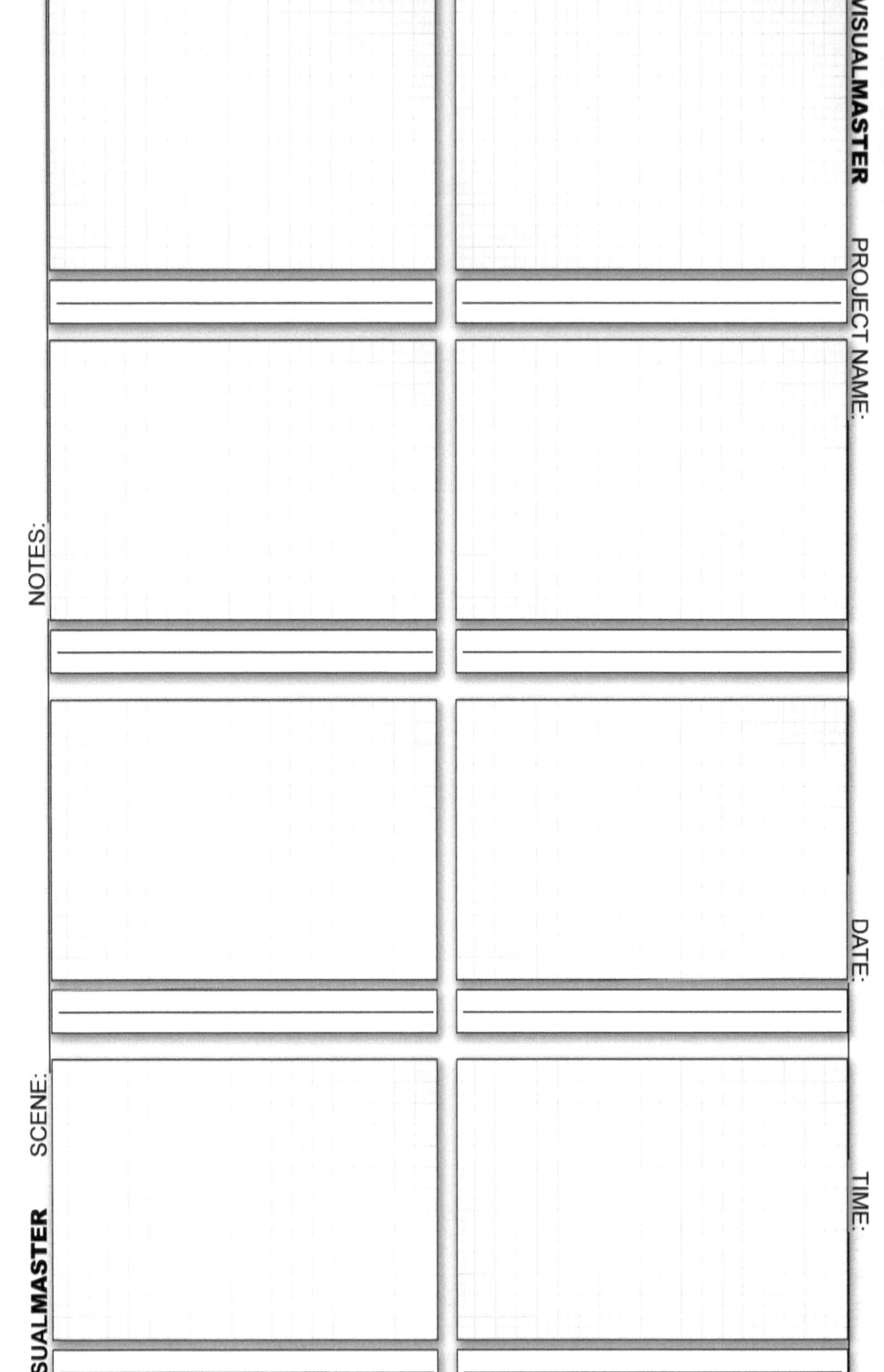

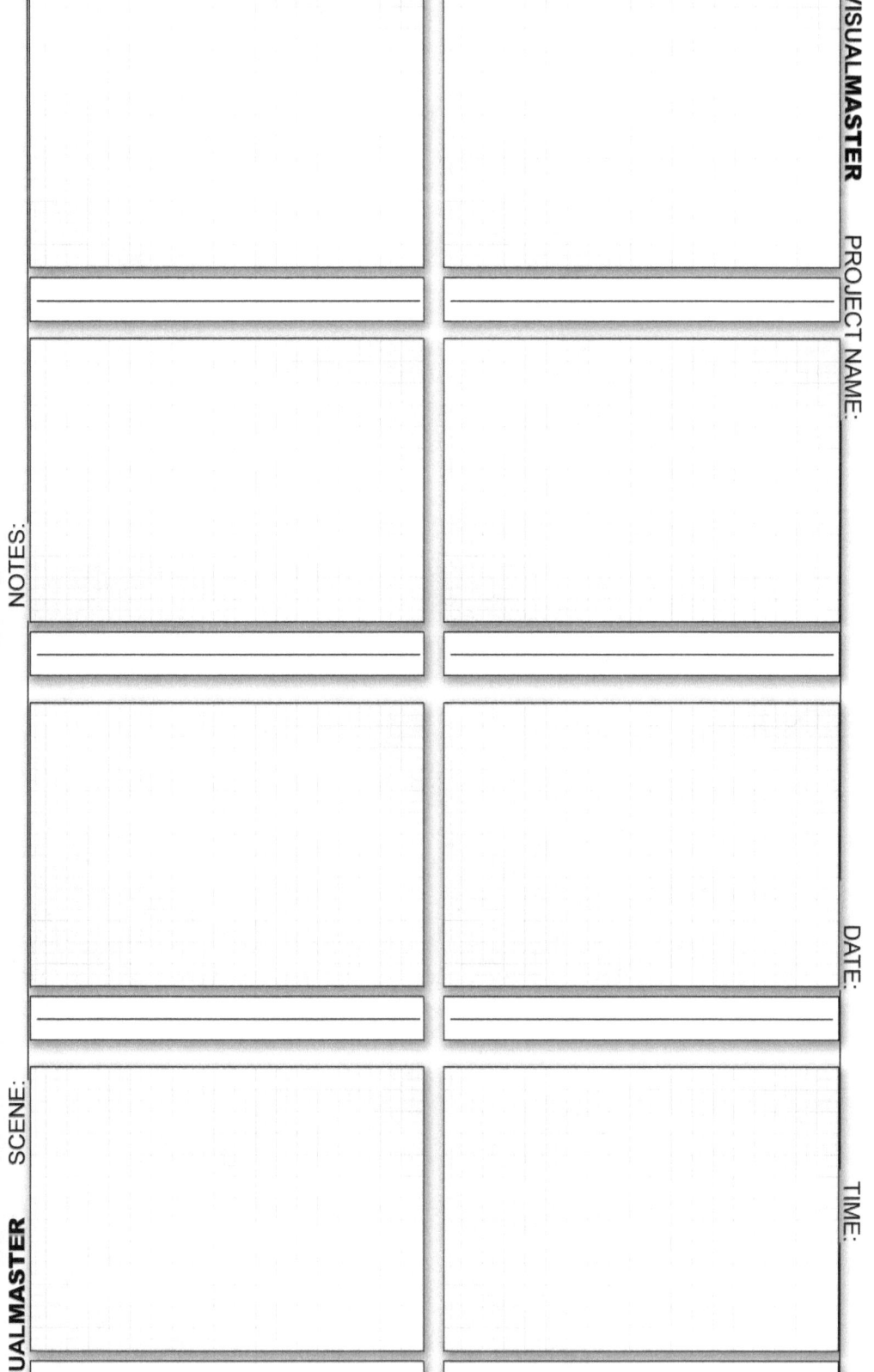

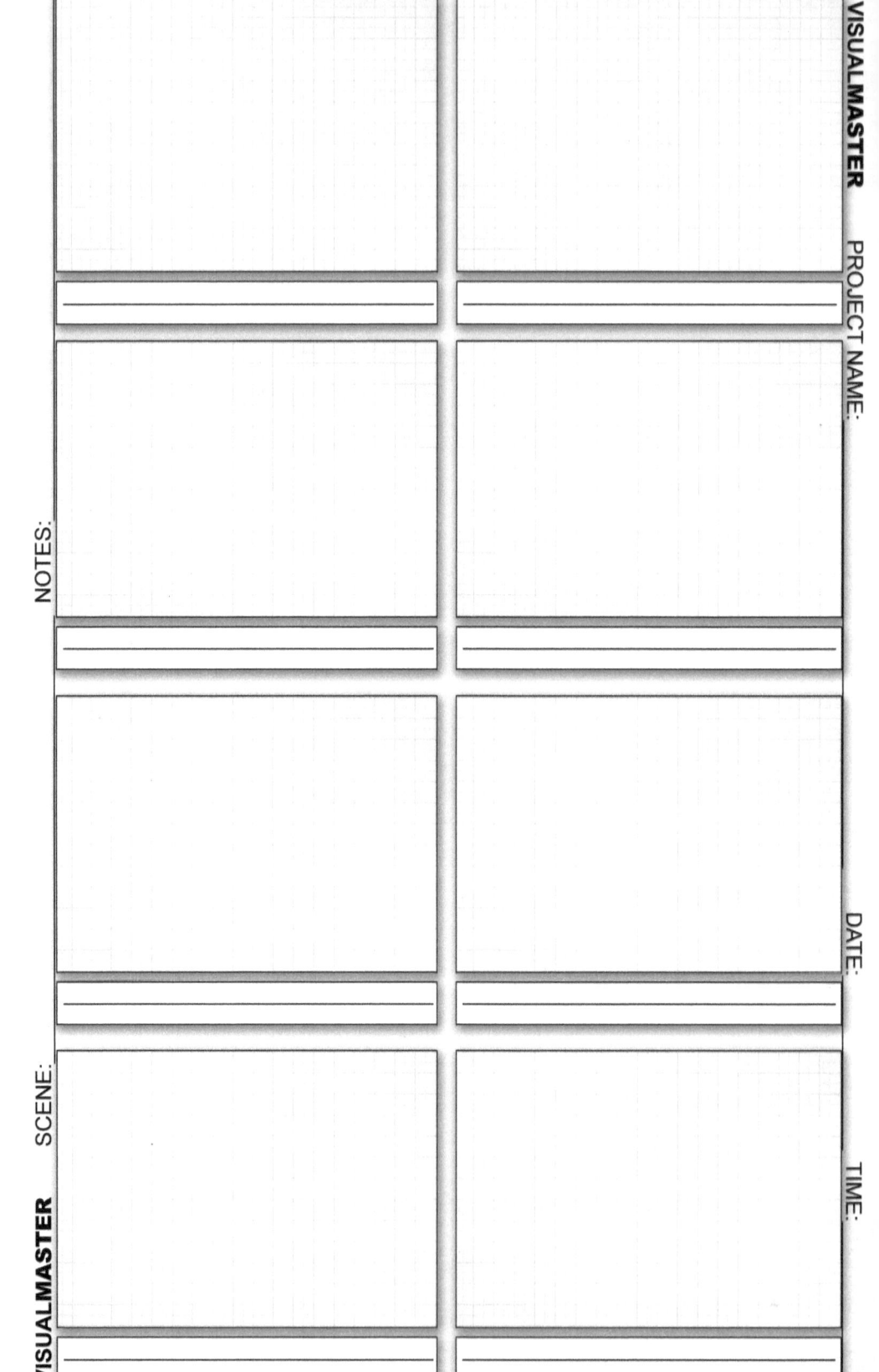

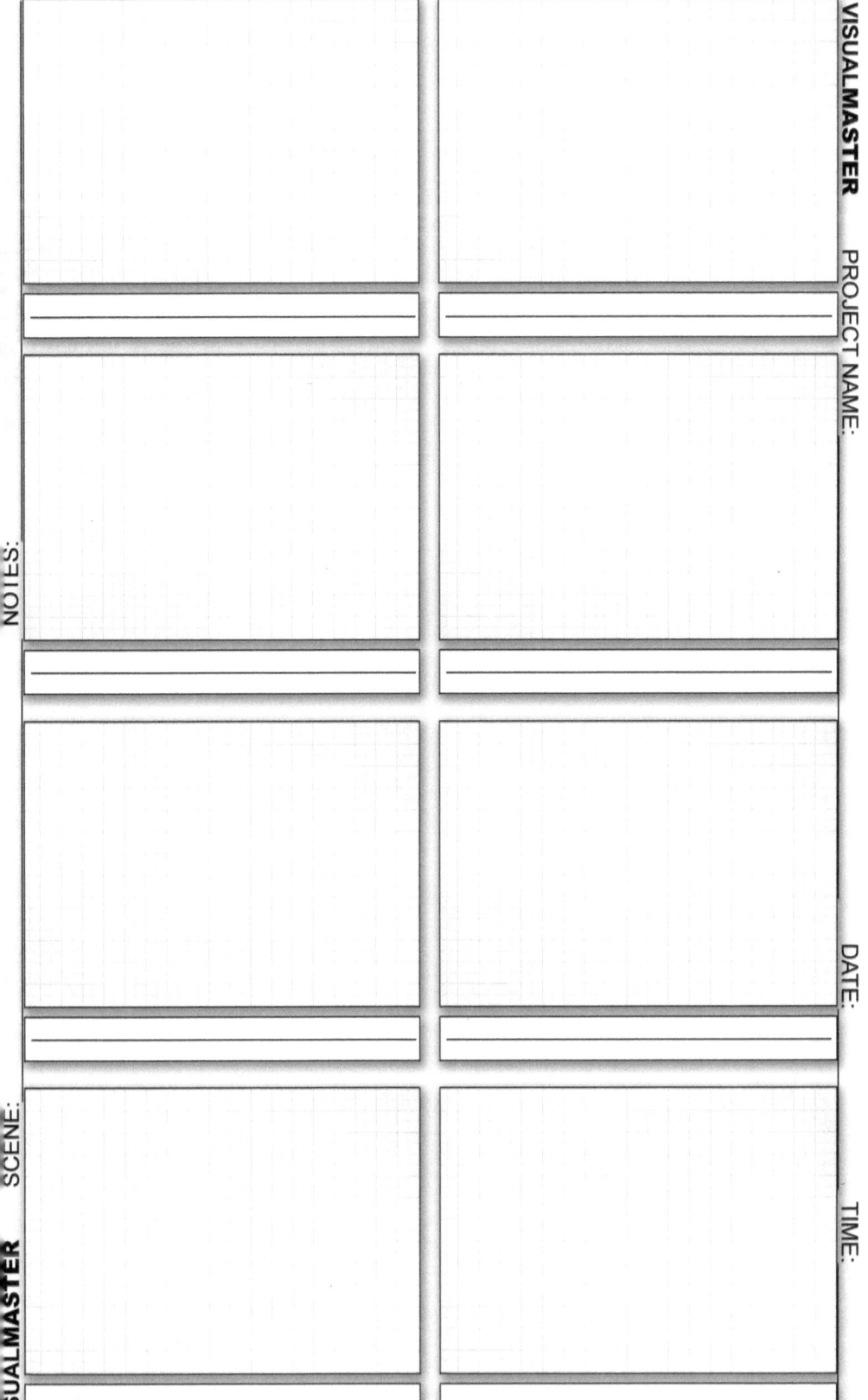

VISUALMASTER

PROJECT NAME:

DATE:

TIME:

NOTES:

SCENE:

VISUALMASTER

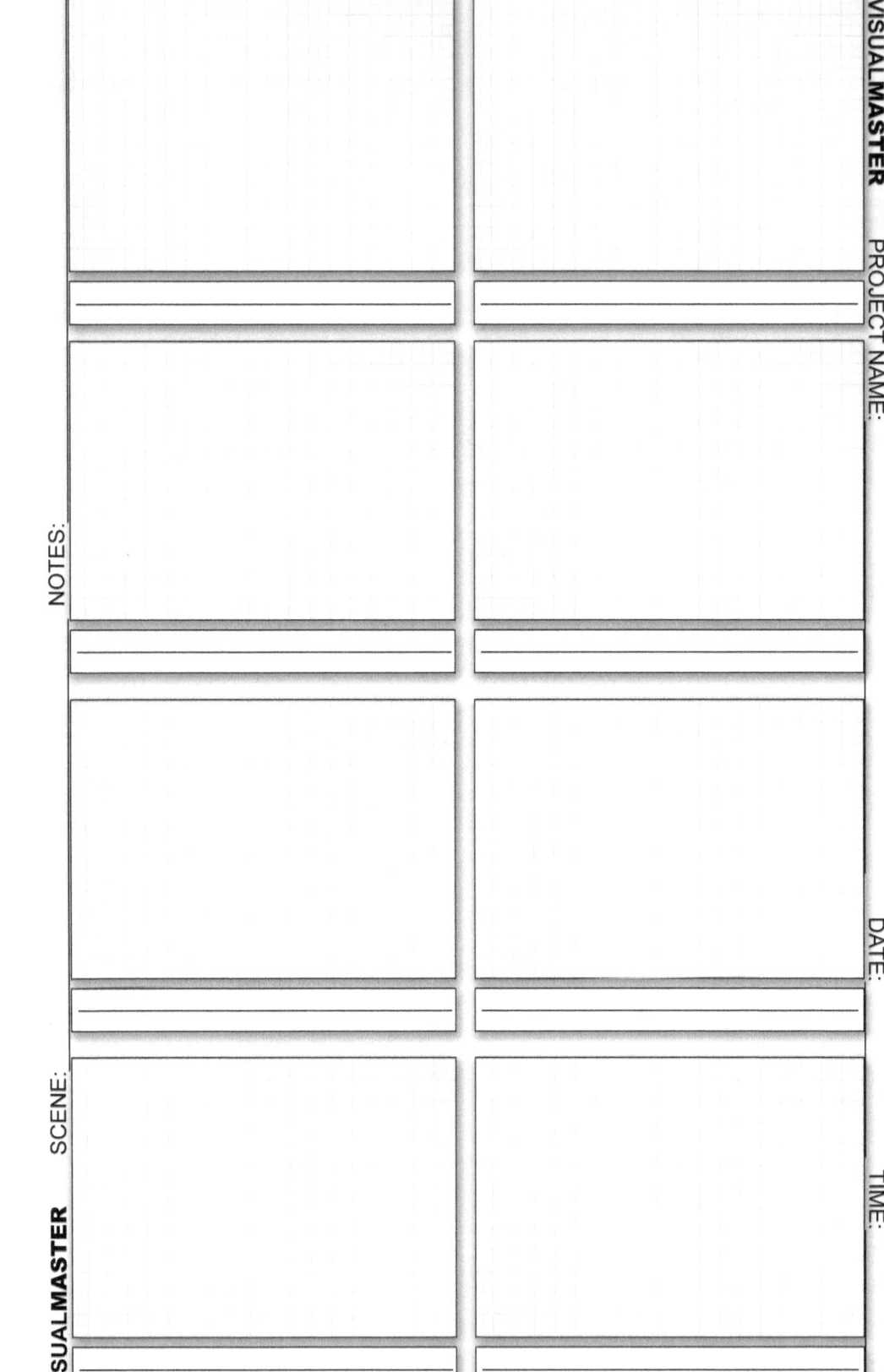

VISUALMASTER

PROJECT NAME:

DATE:

TIME:

NOTES:

SCENE:

VISUALMASTER

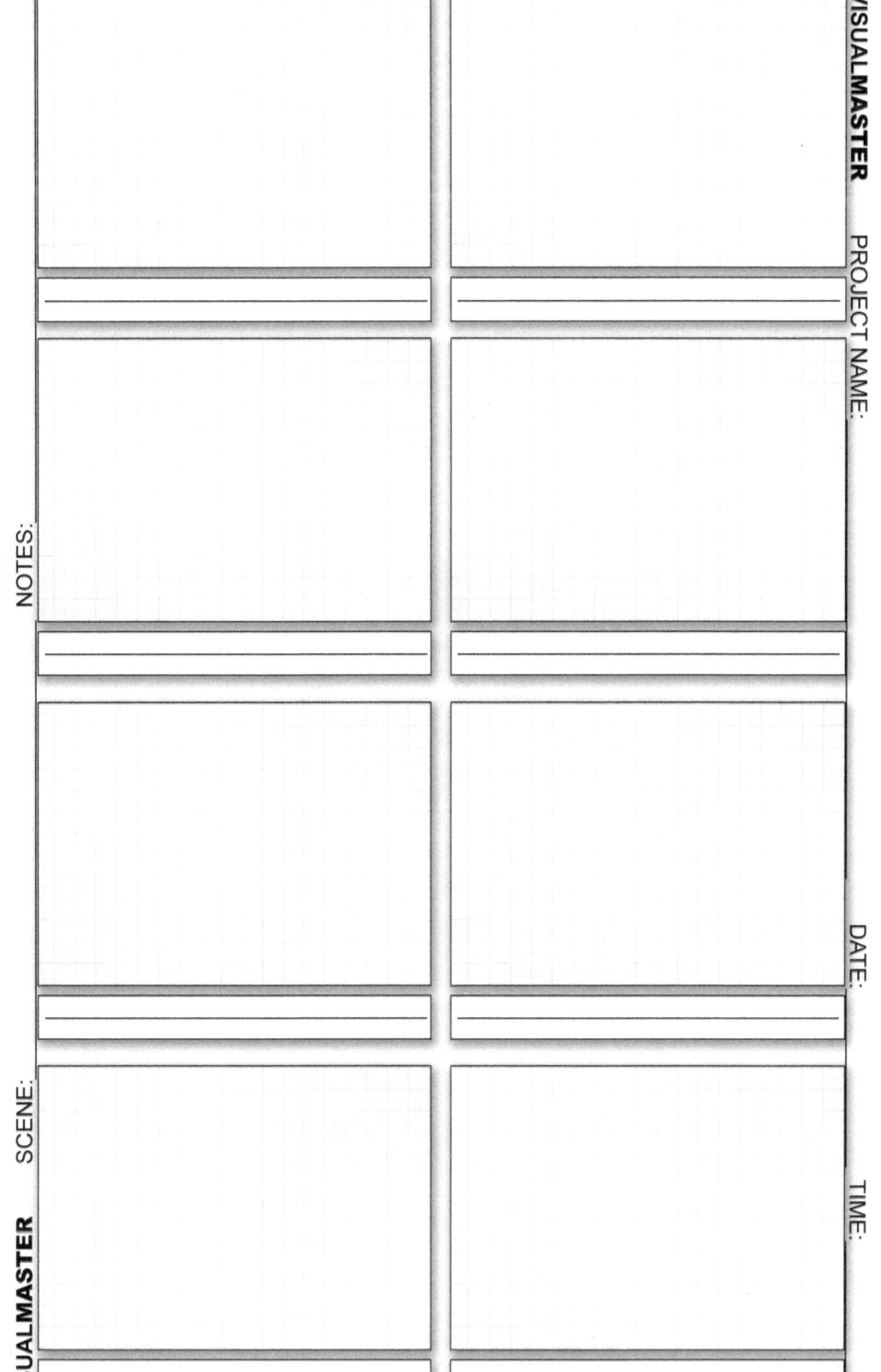

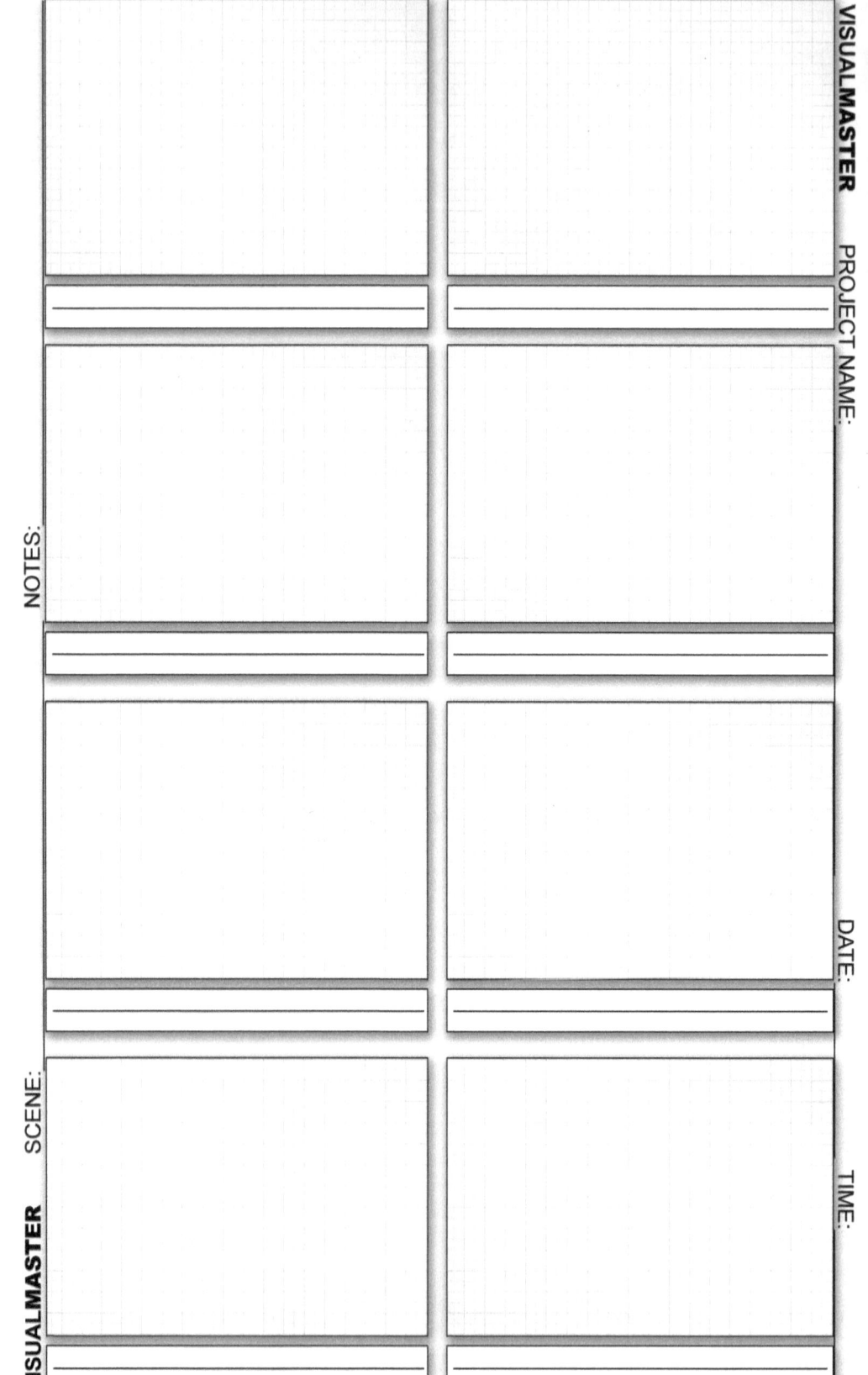

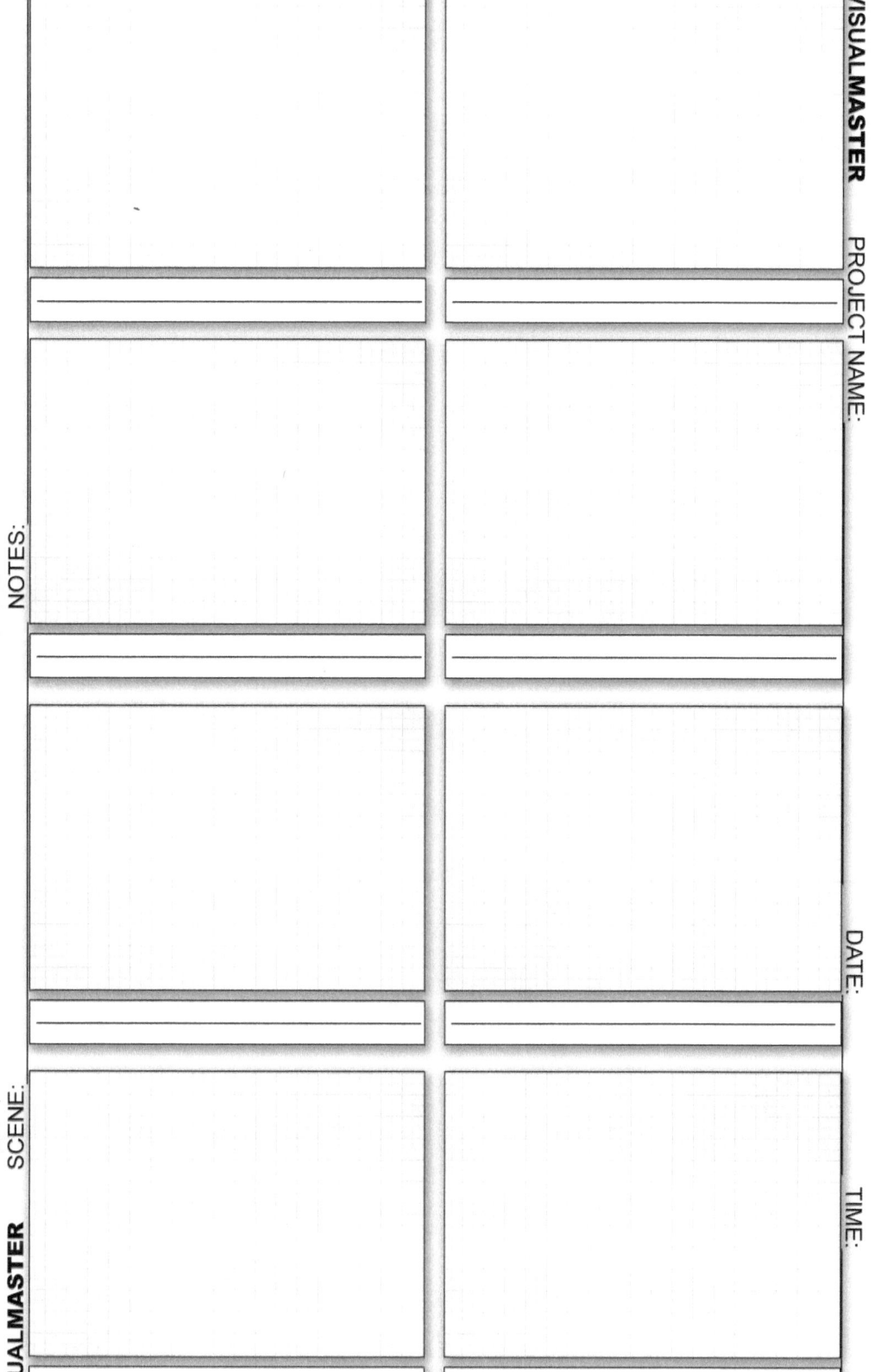

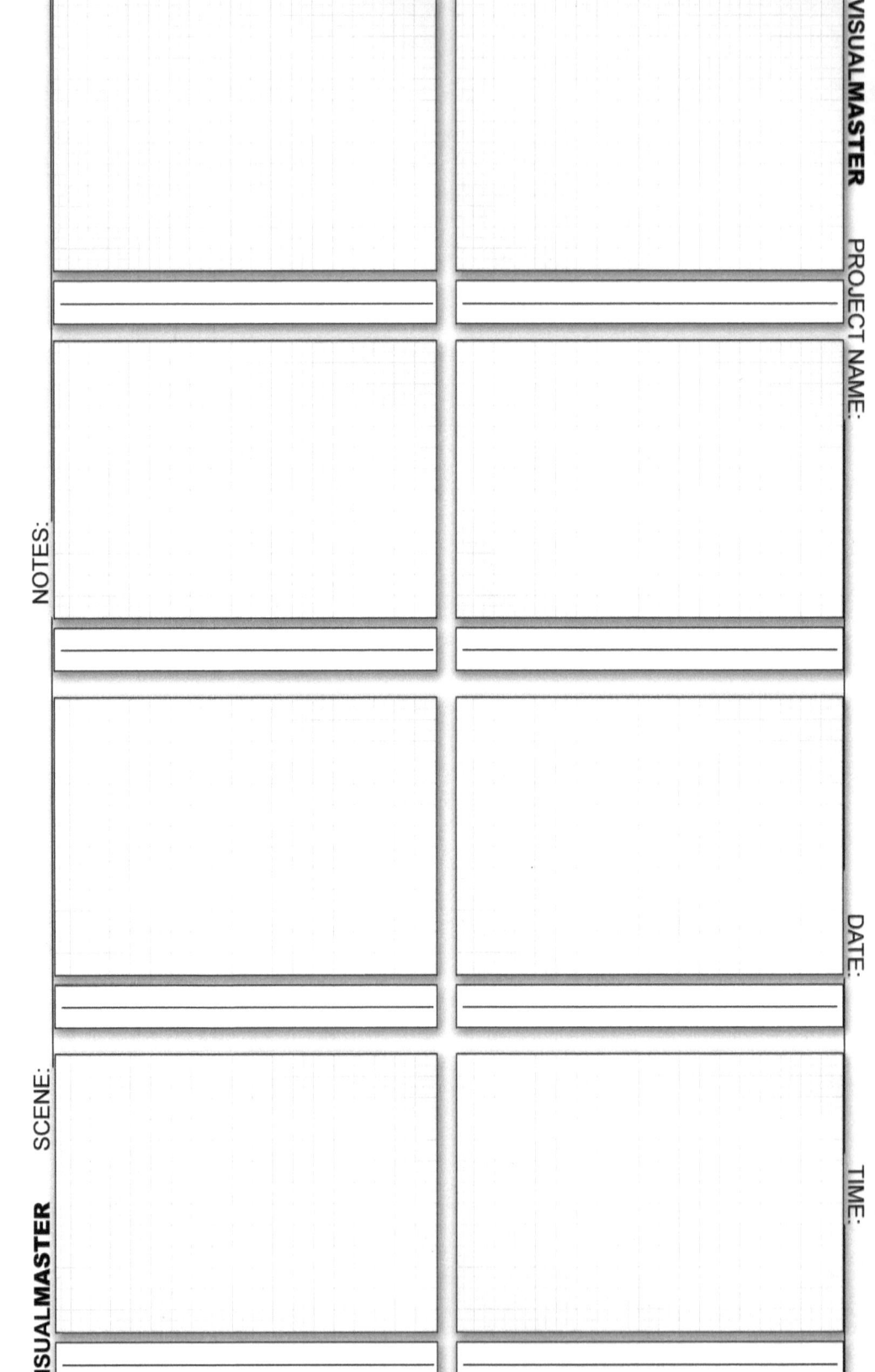

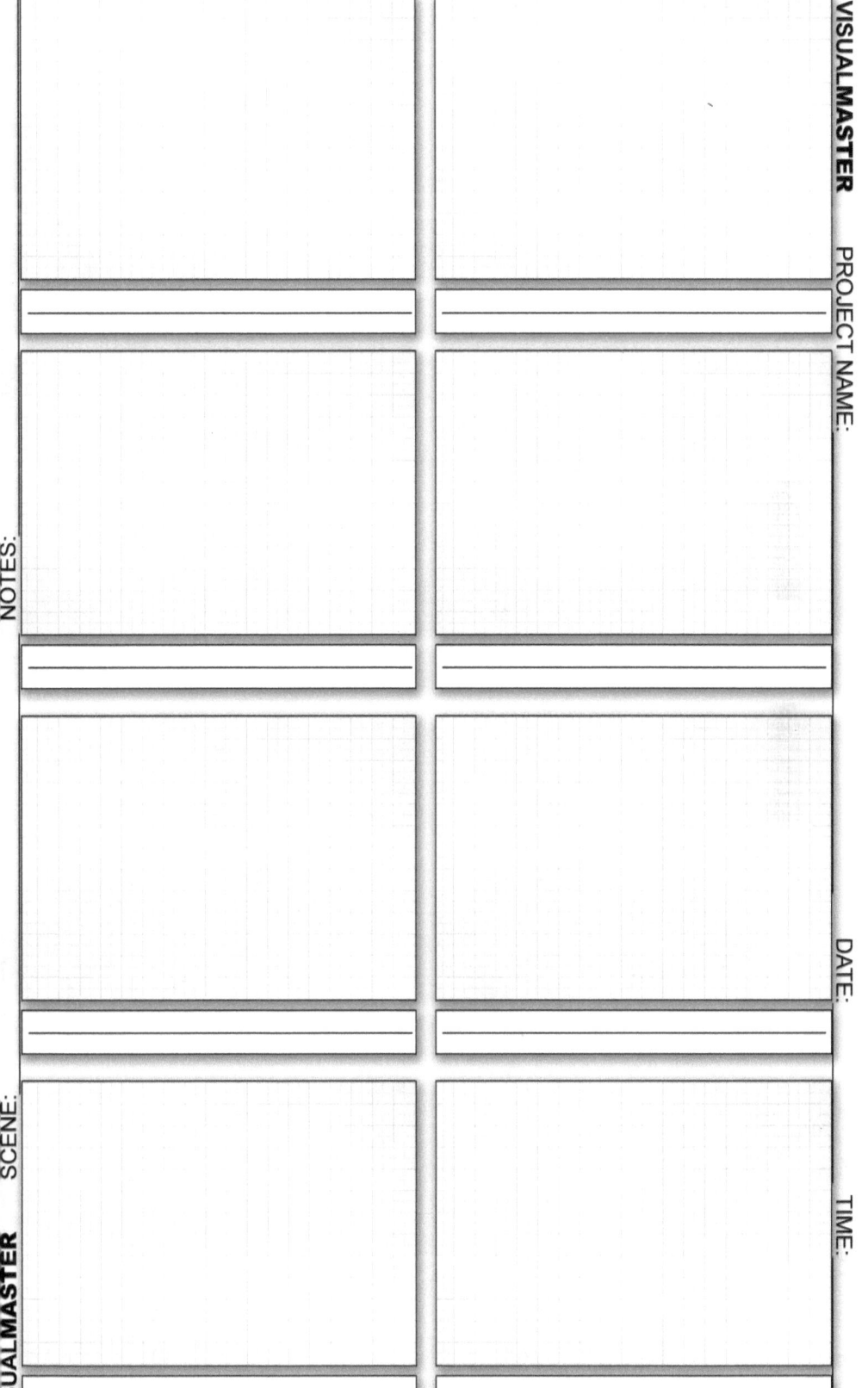

VISUALMASTER

PROJECT NAME:

DATE:

TIME:

NOTES:

SCENE:

VISUALMASTER

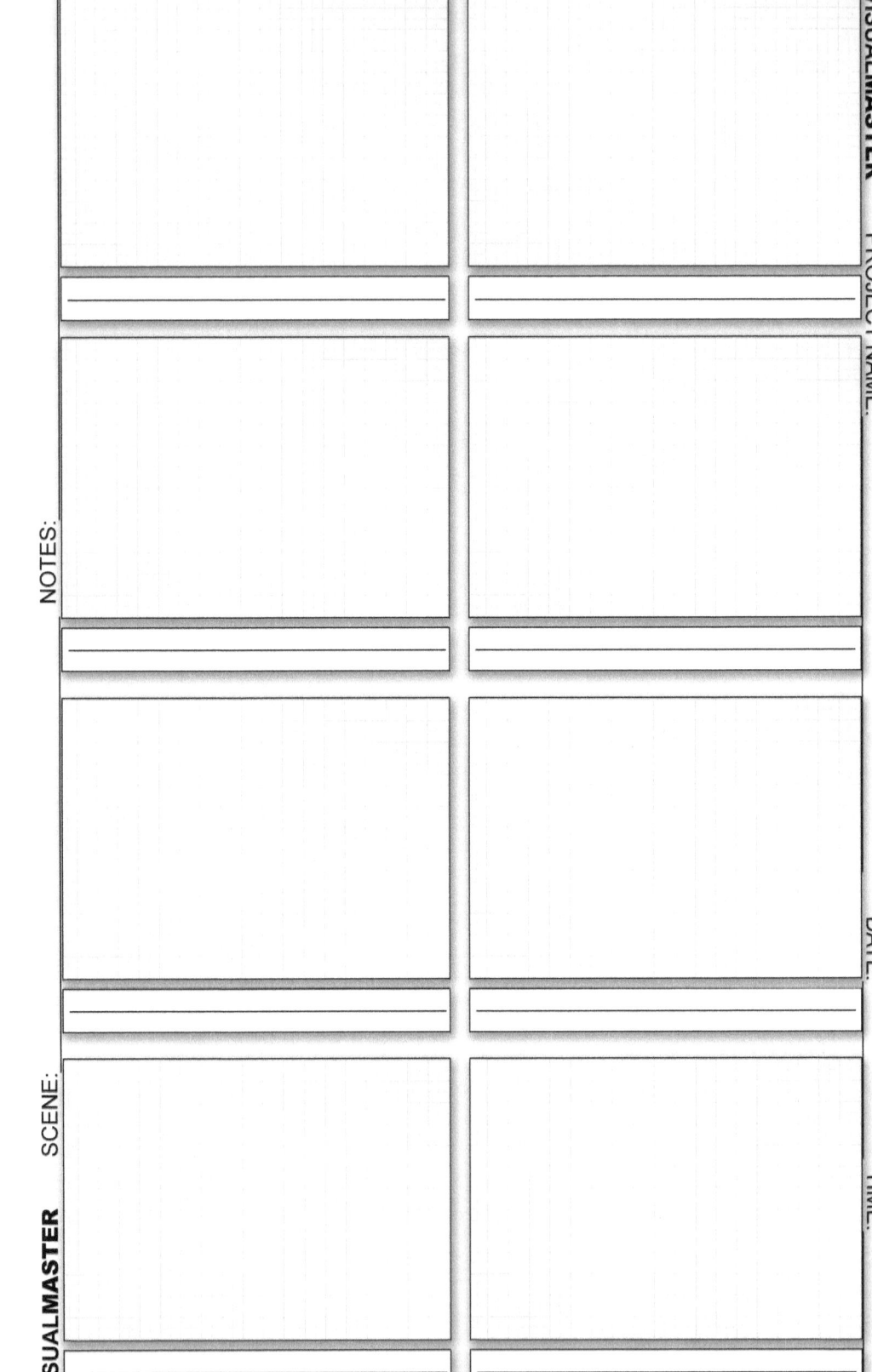

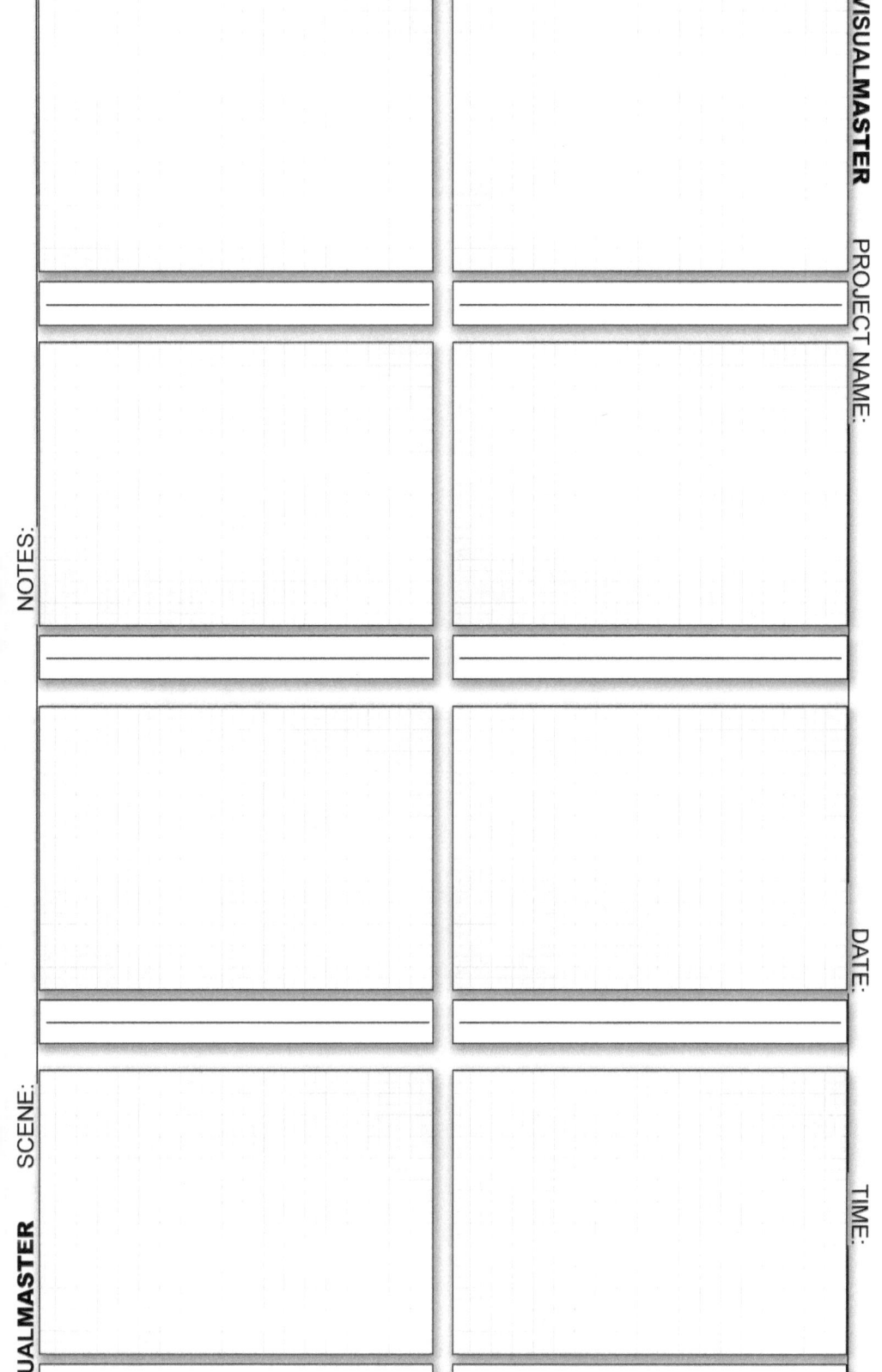

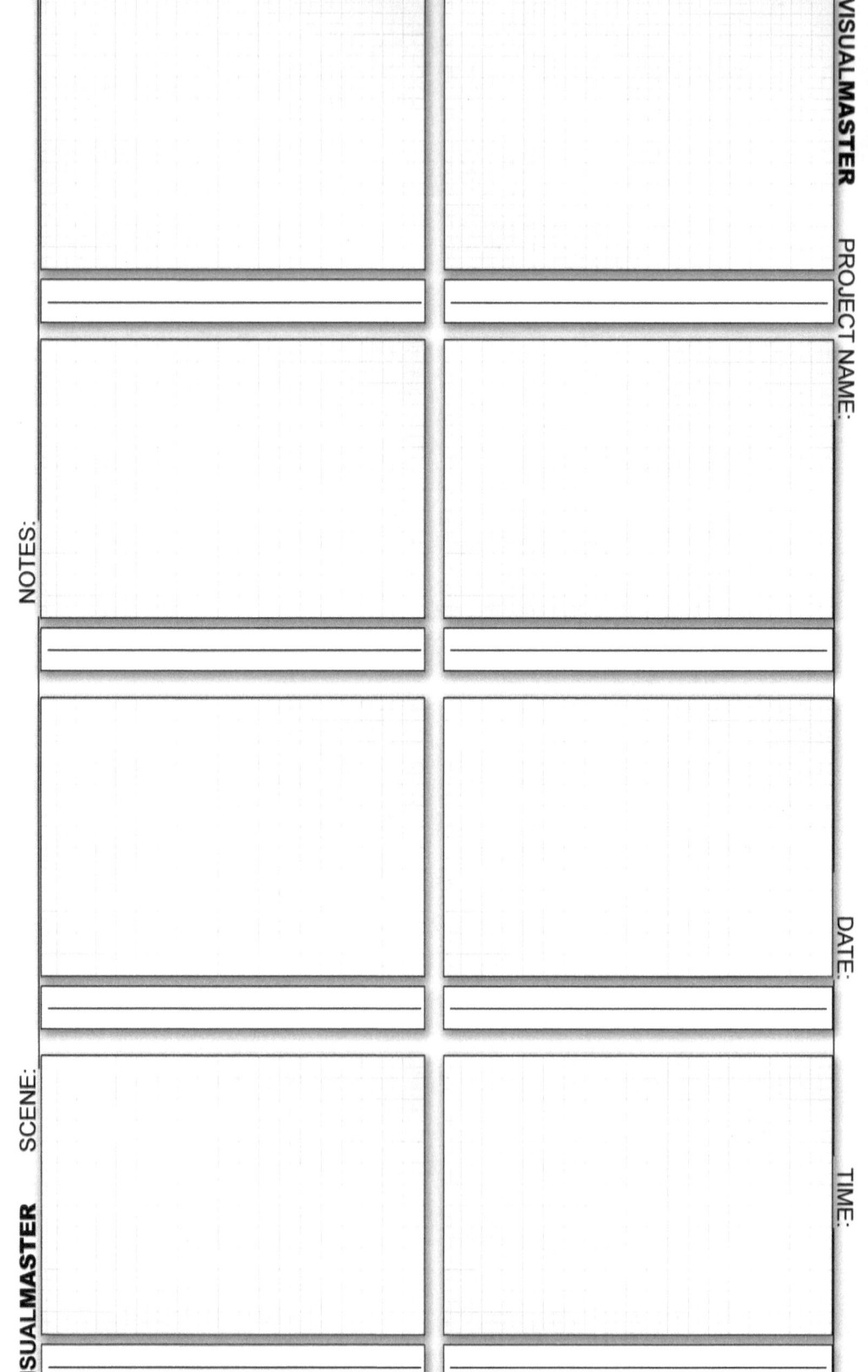

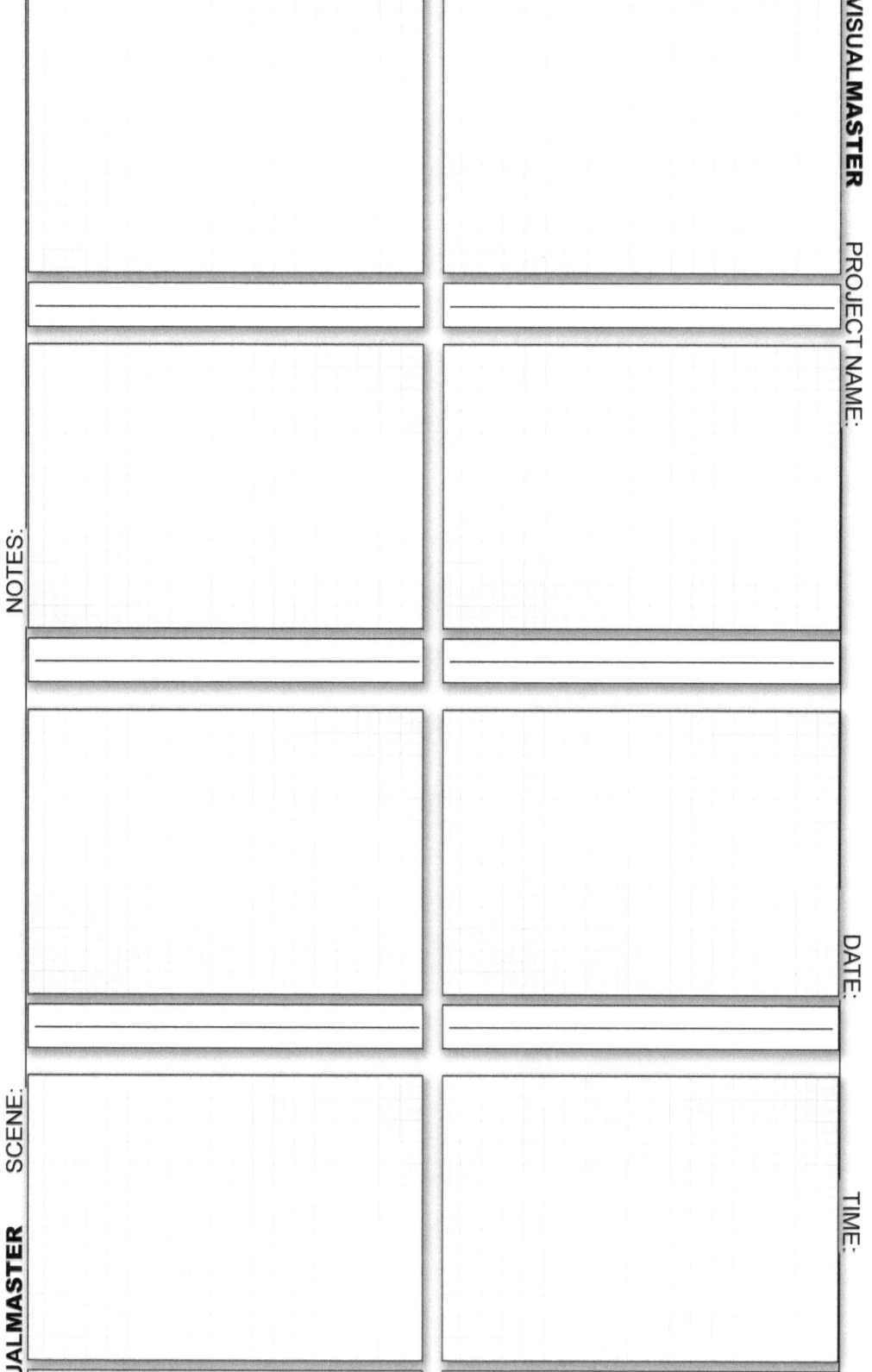

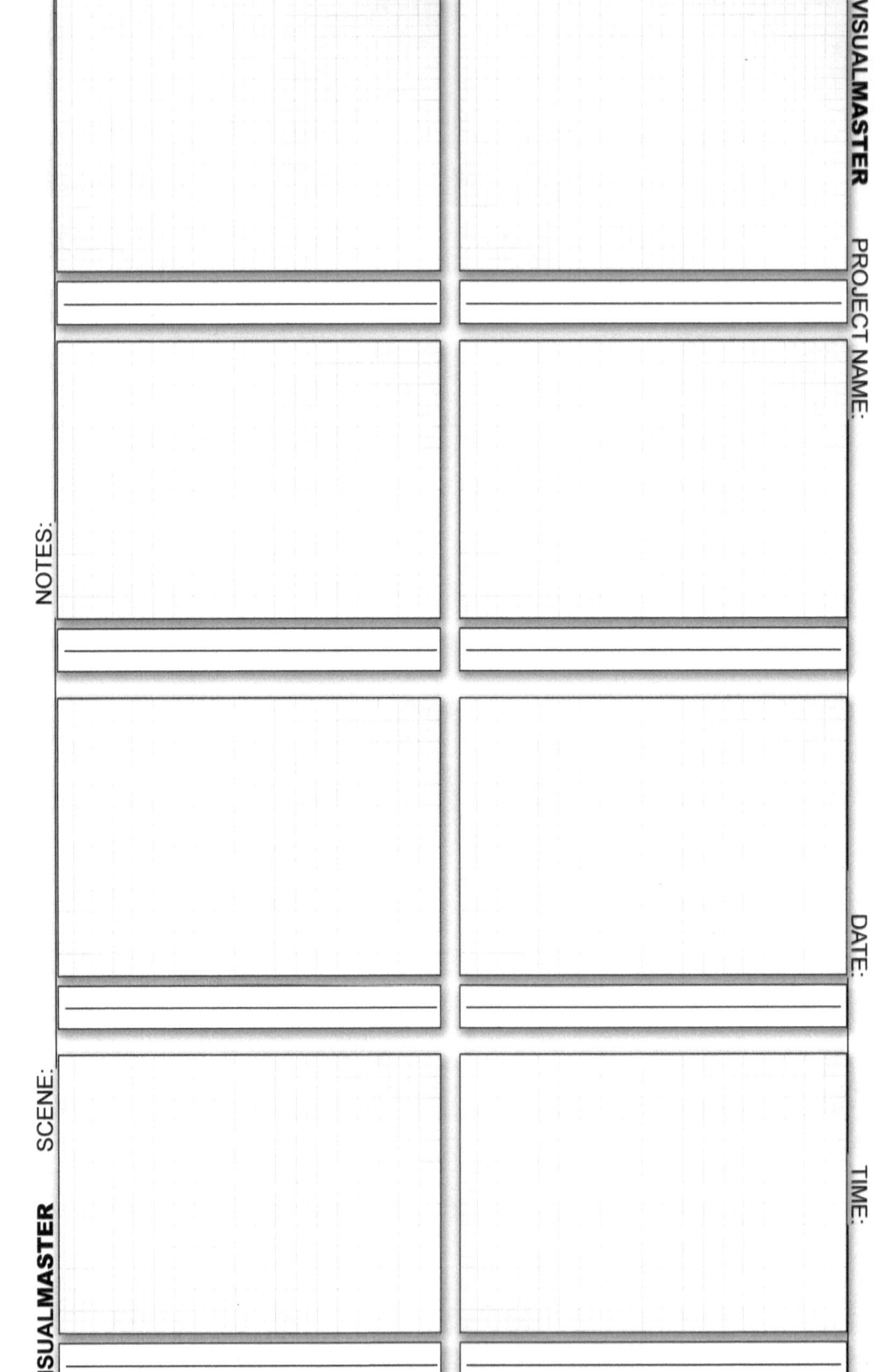

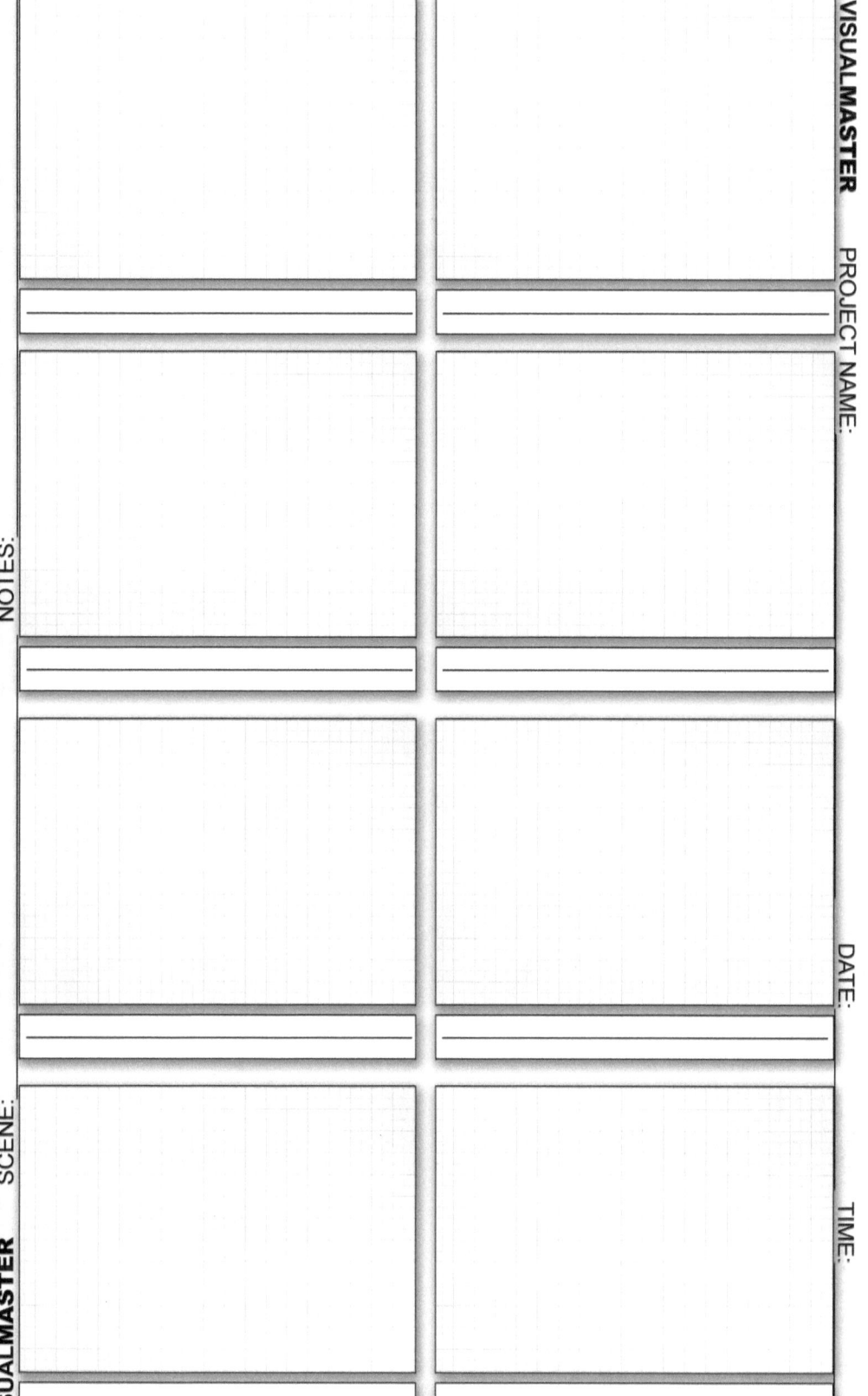

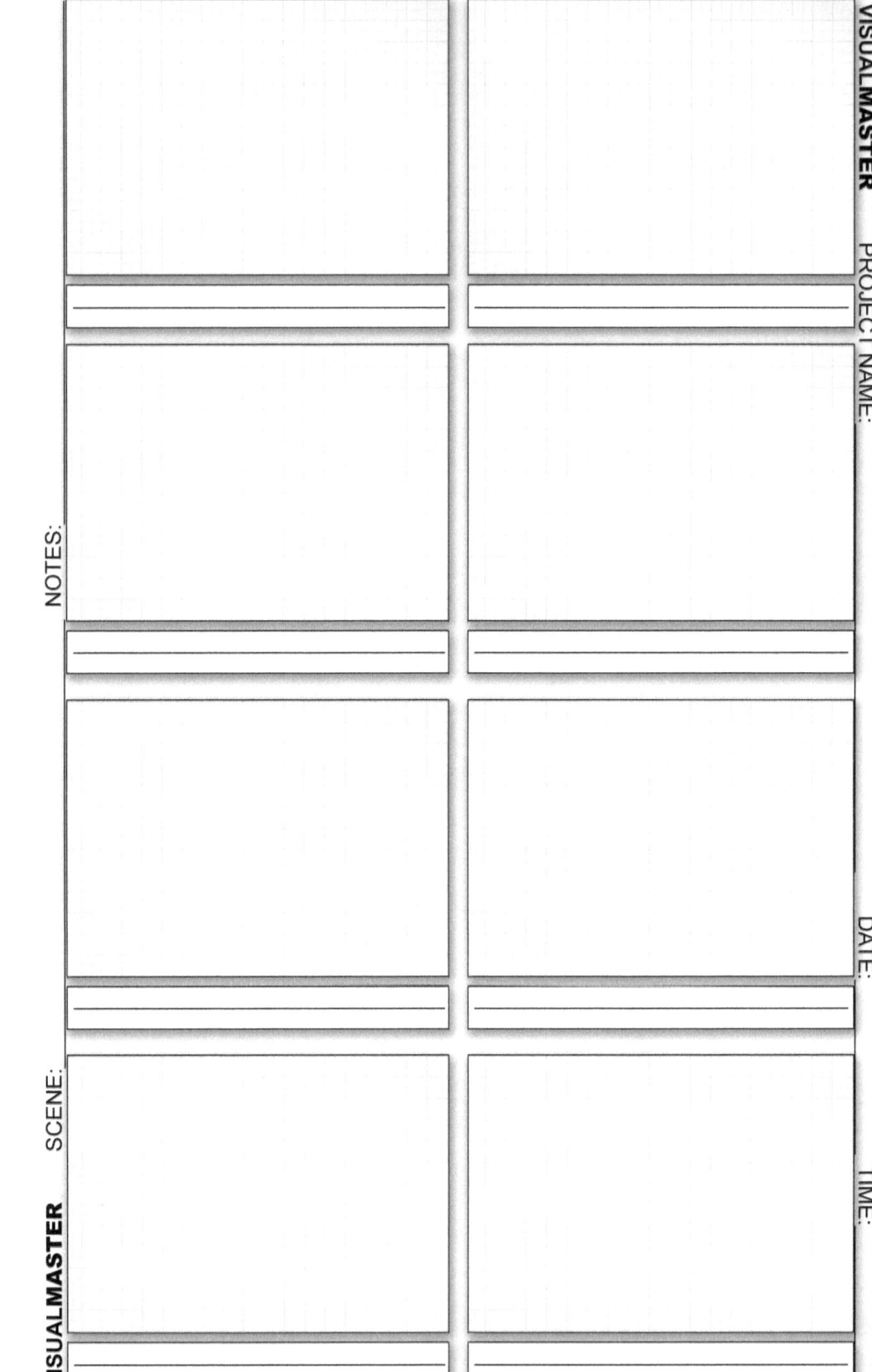

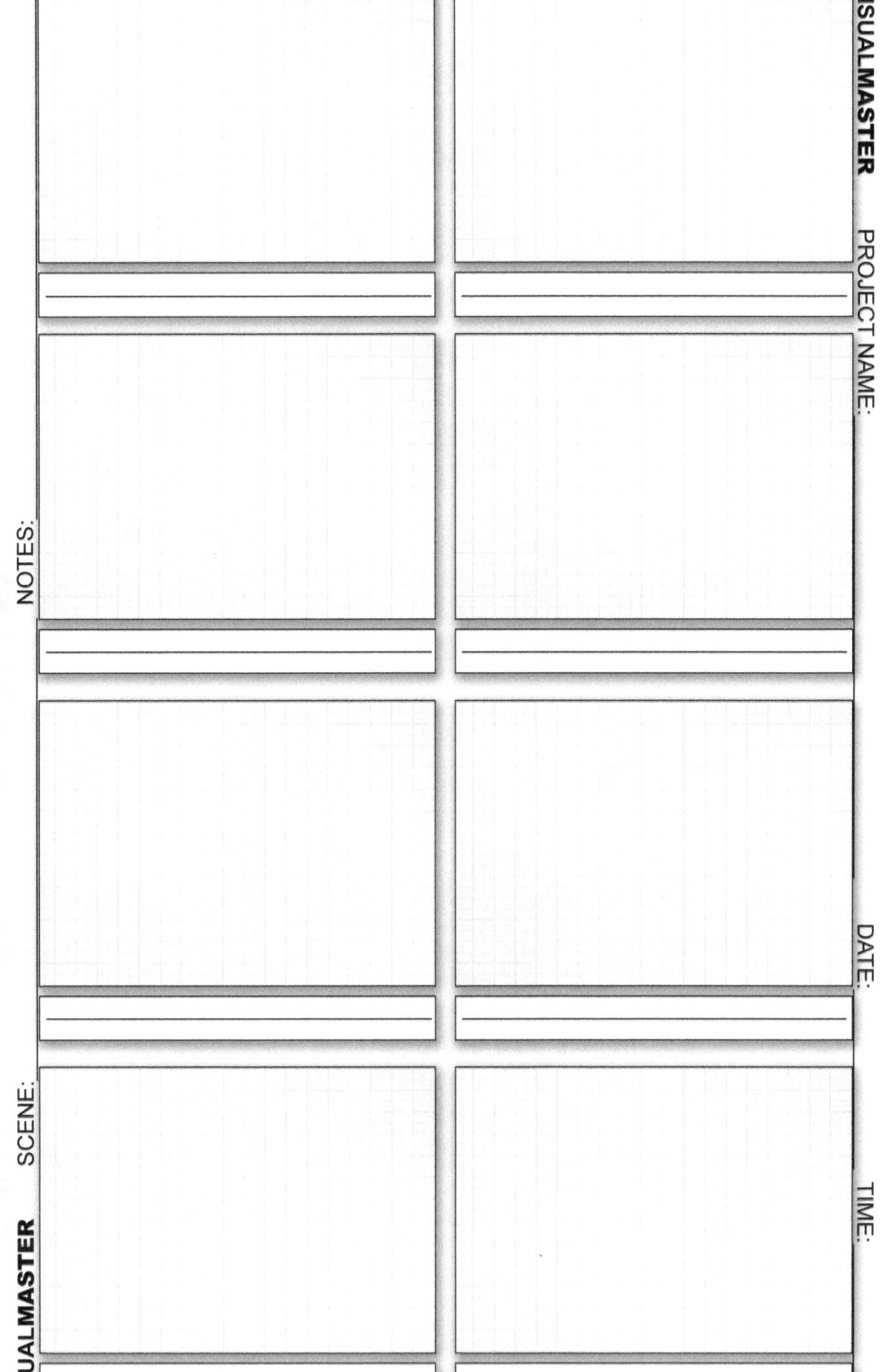

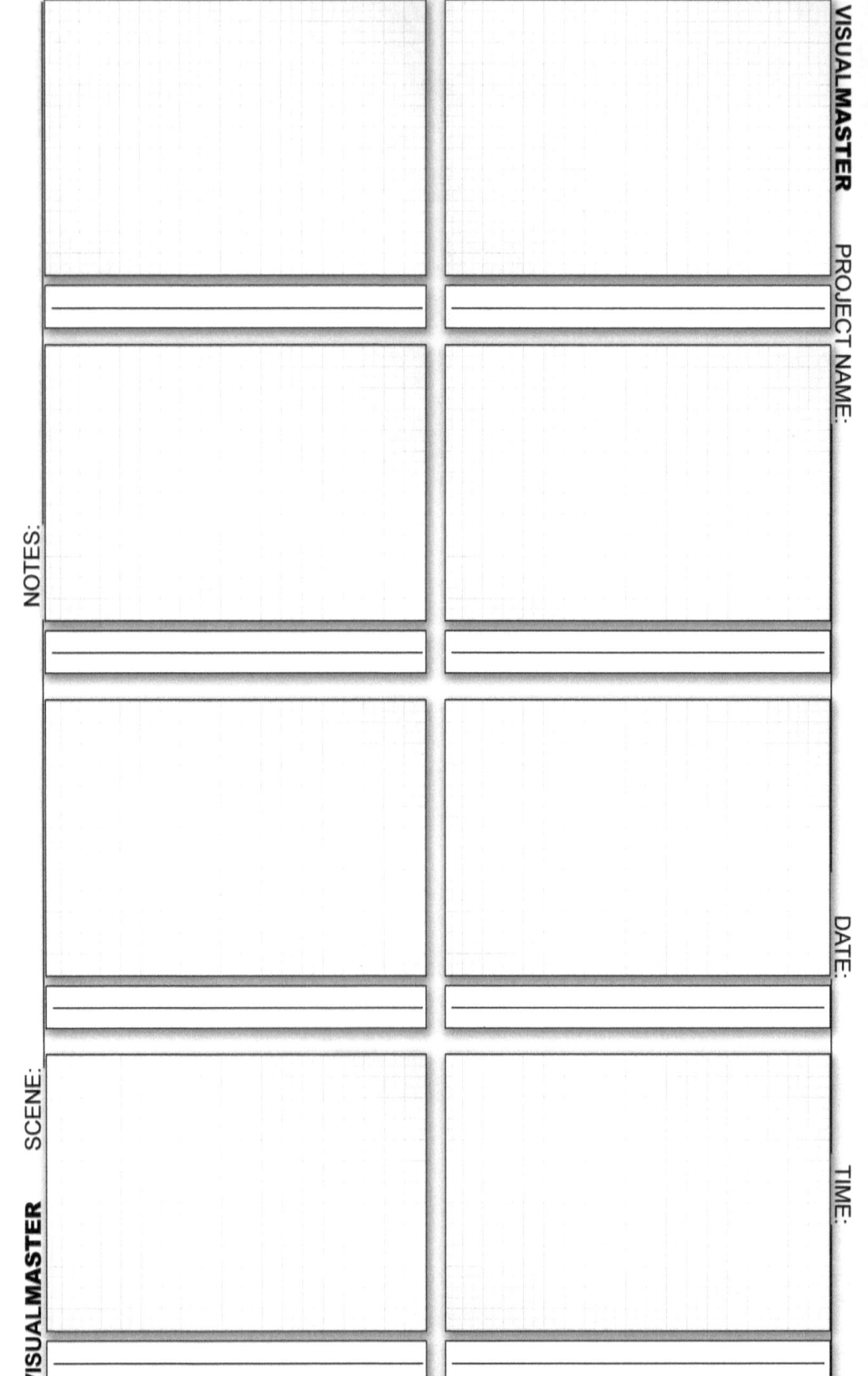

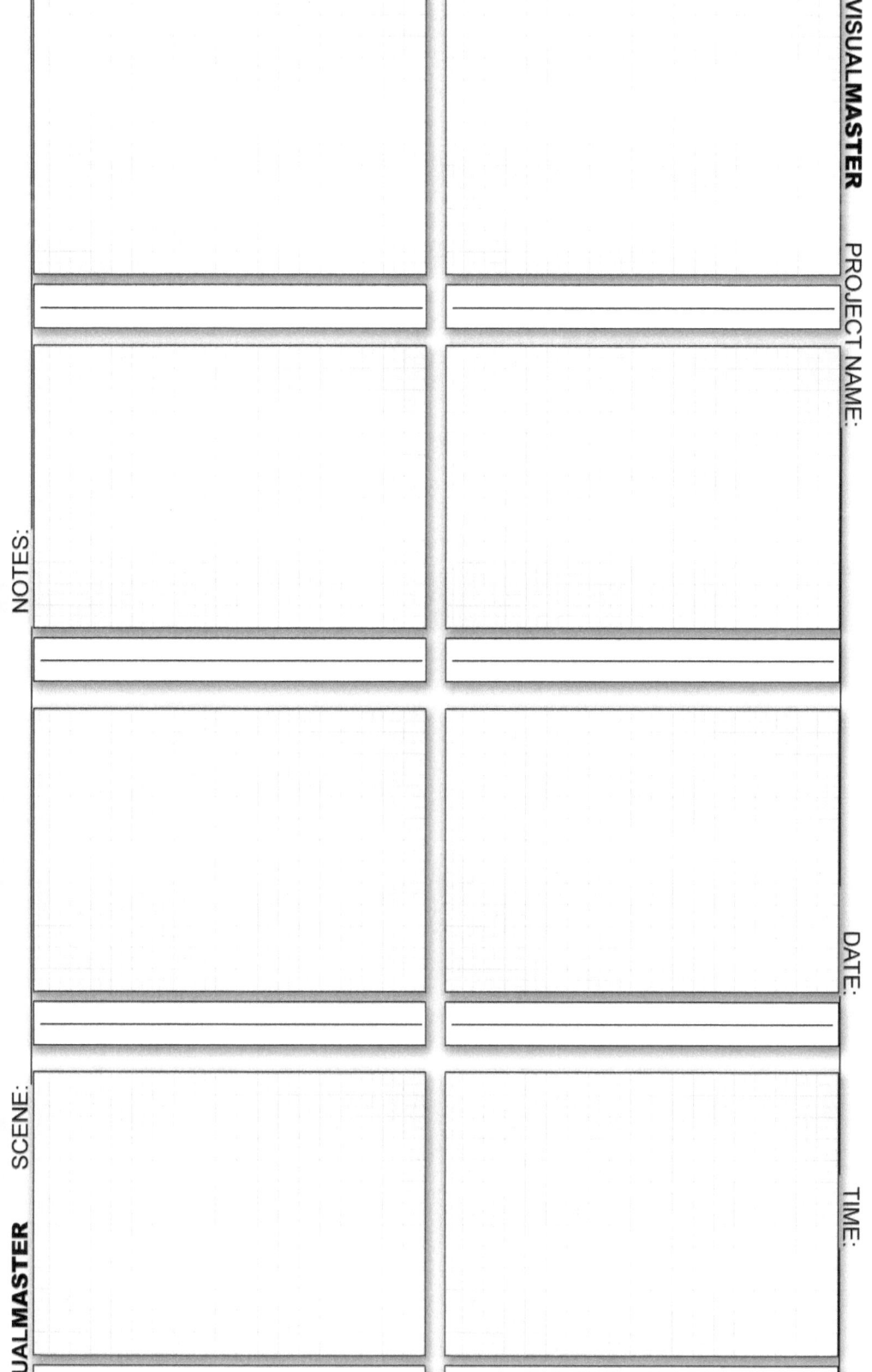

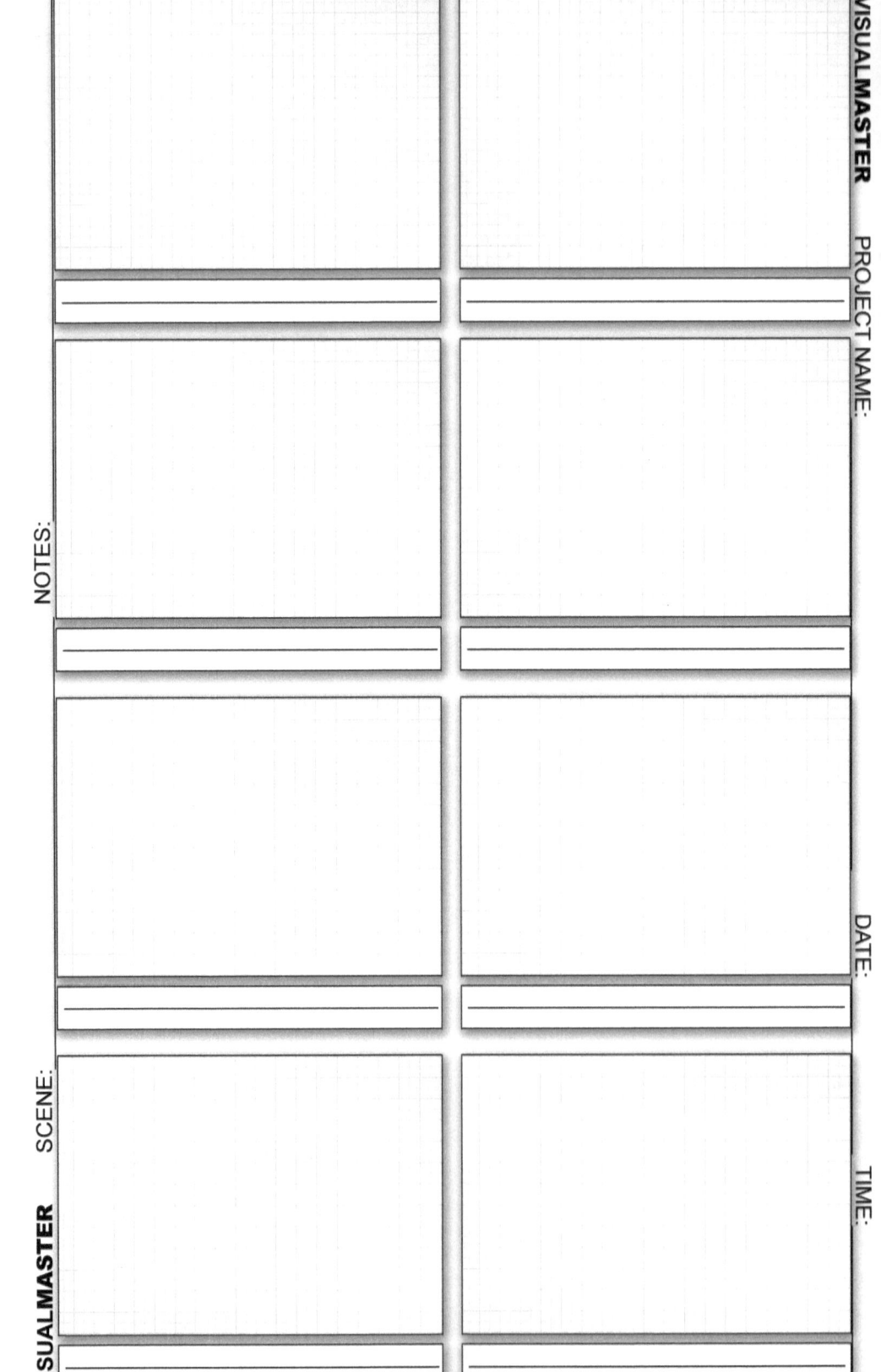

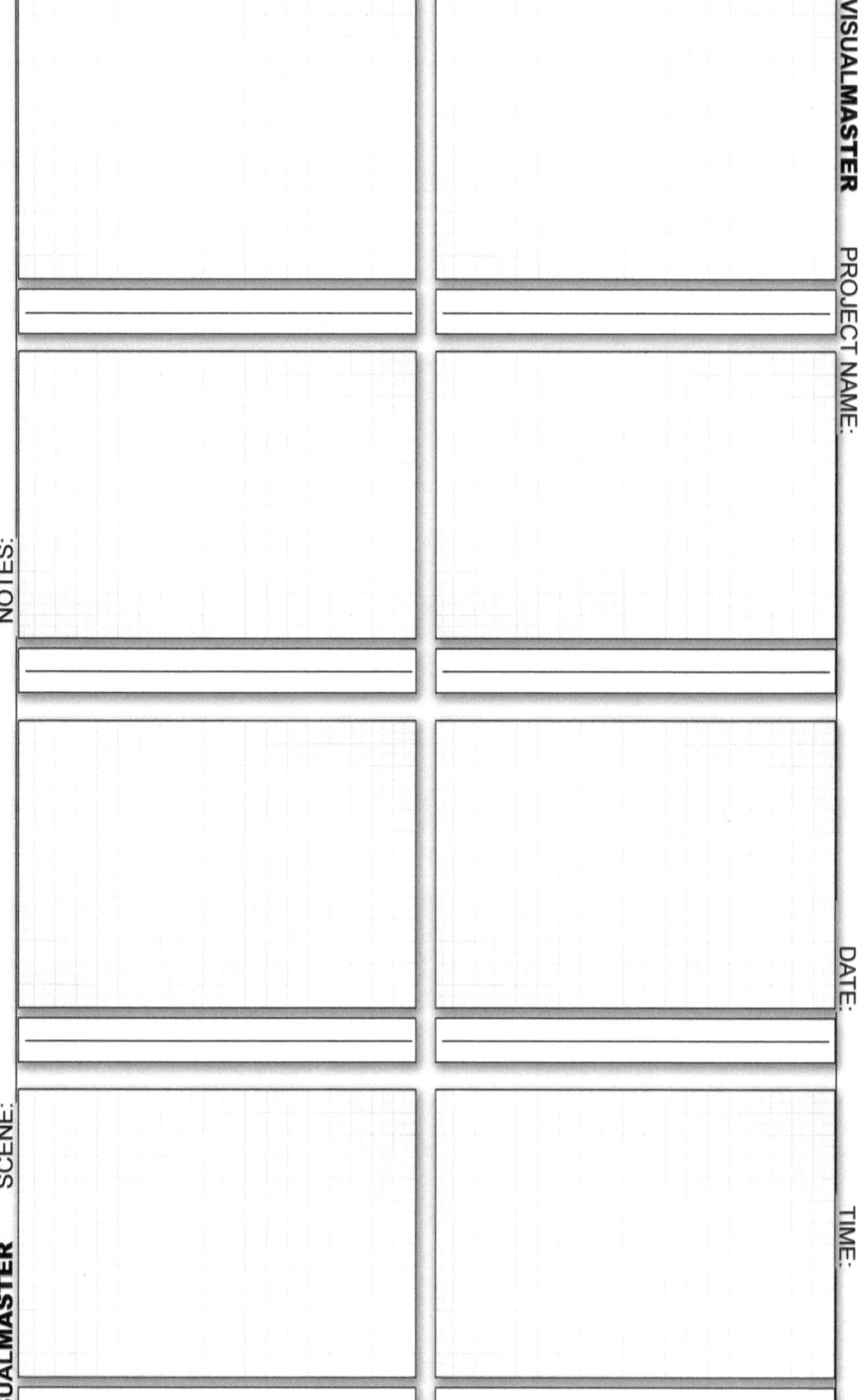

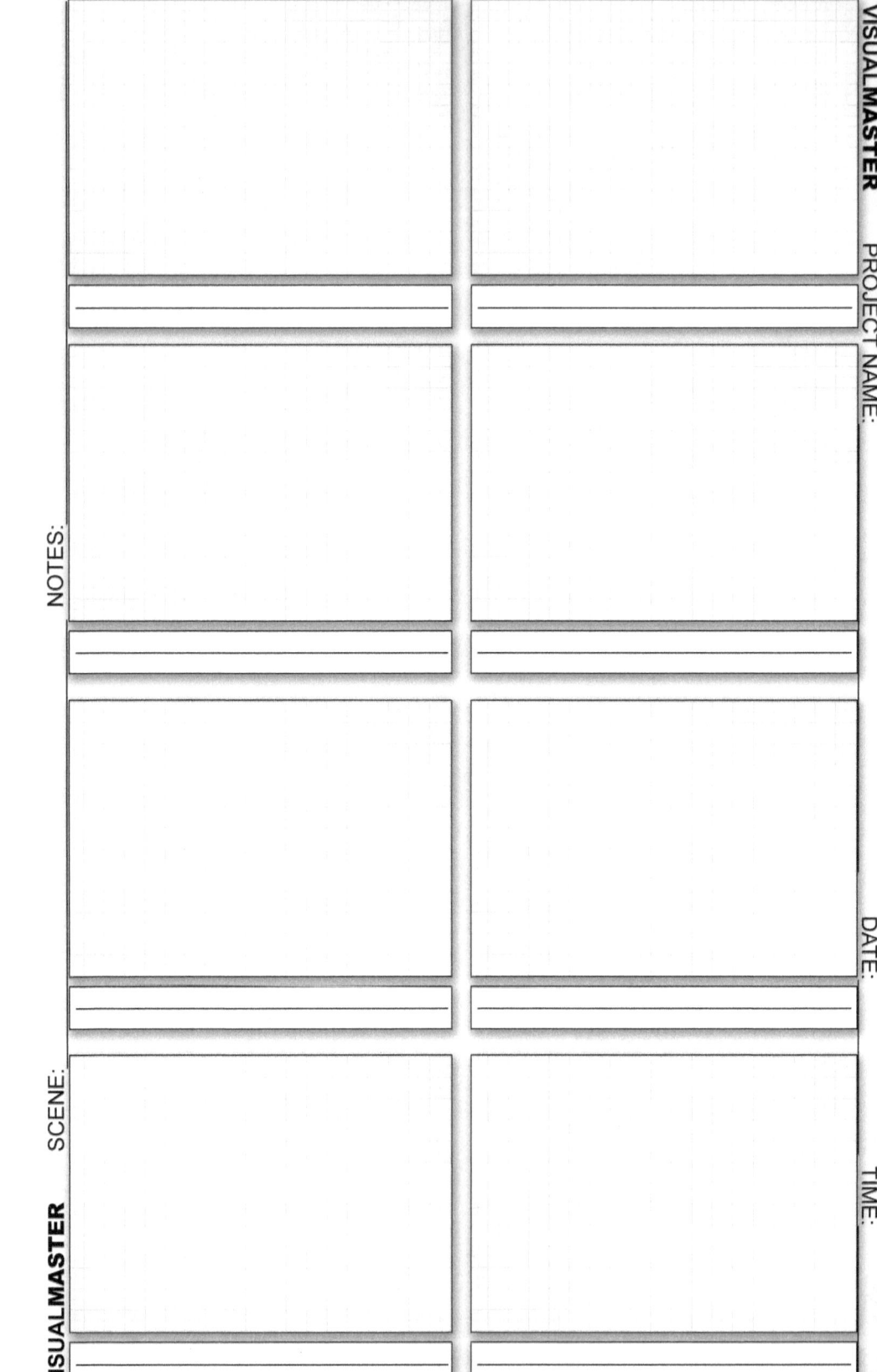

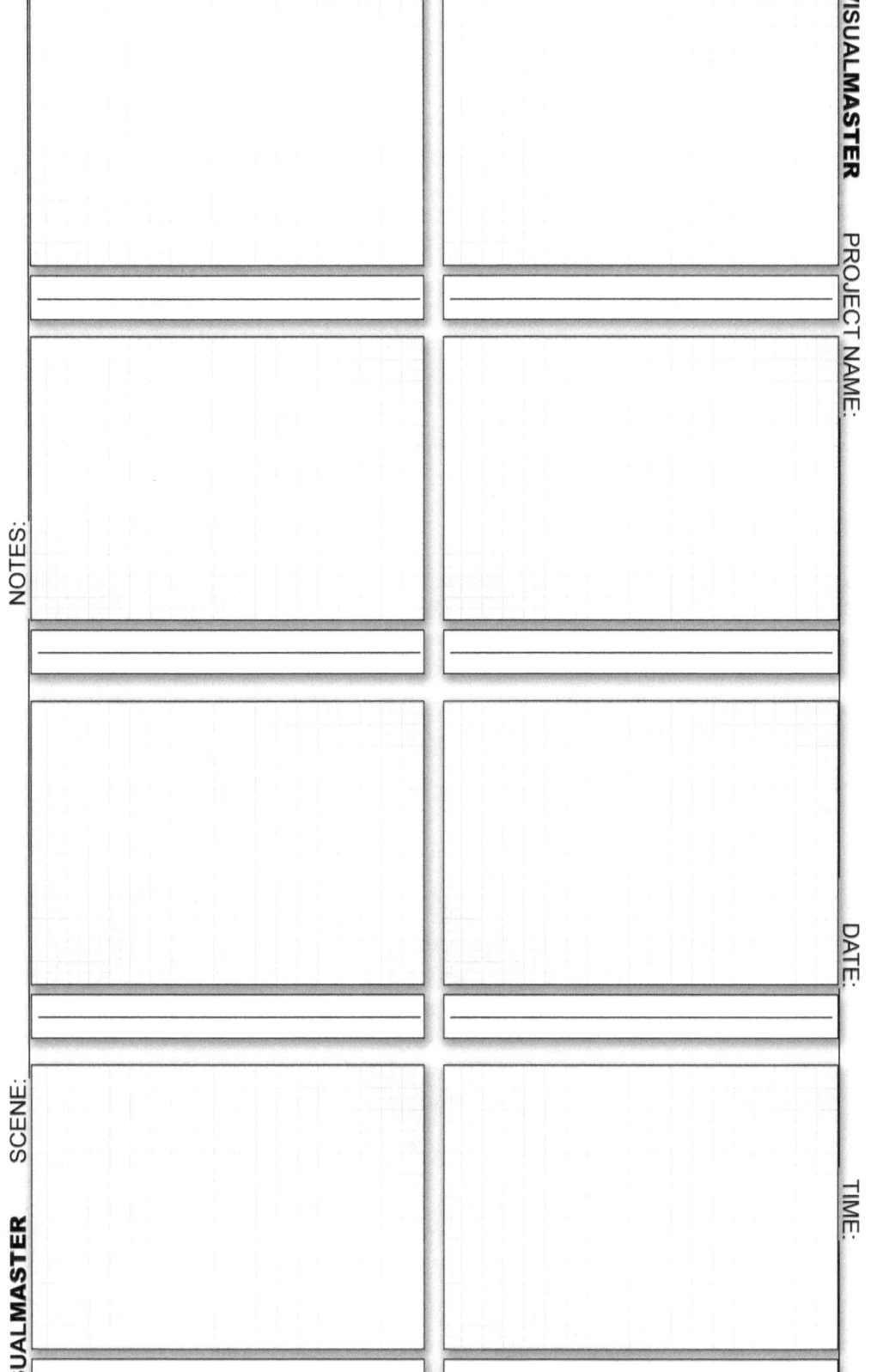

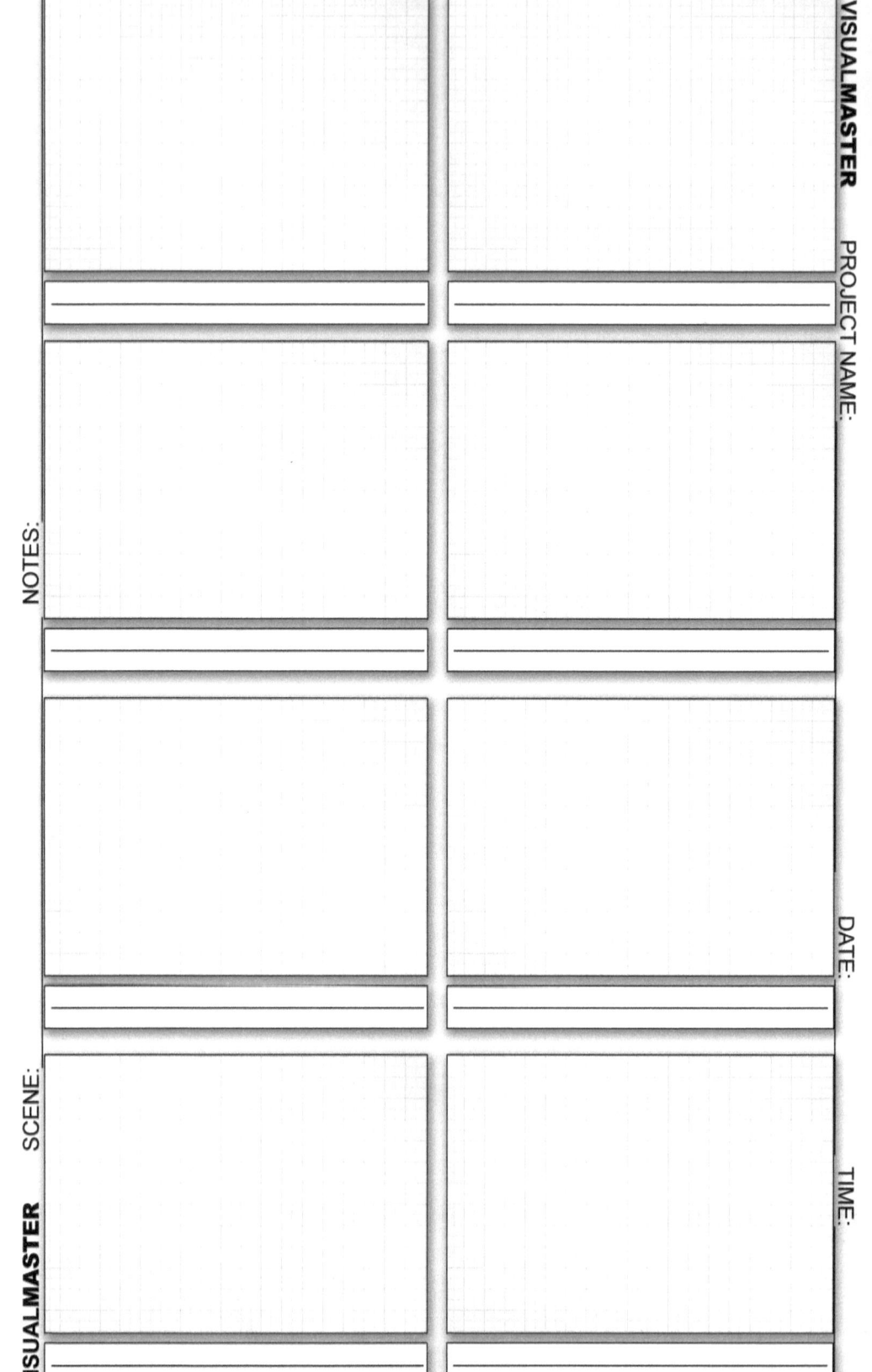

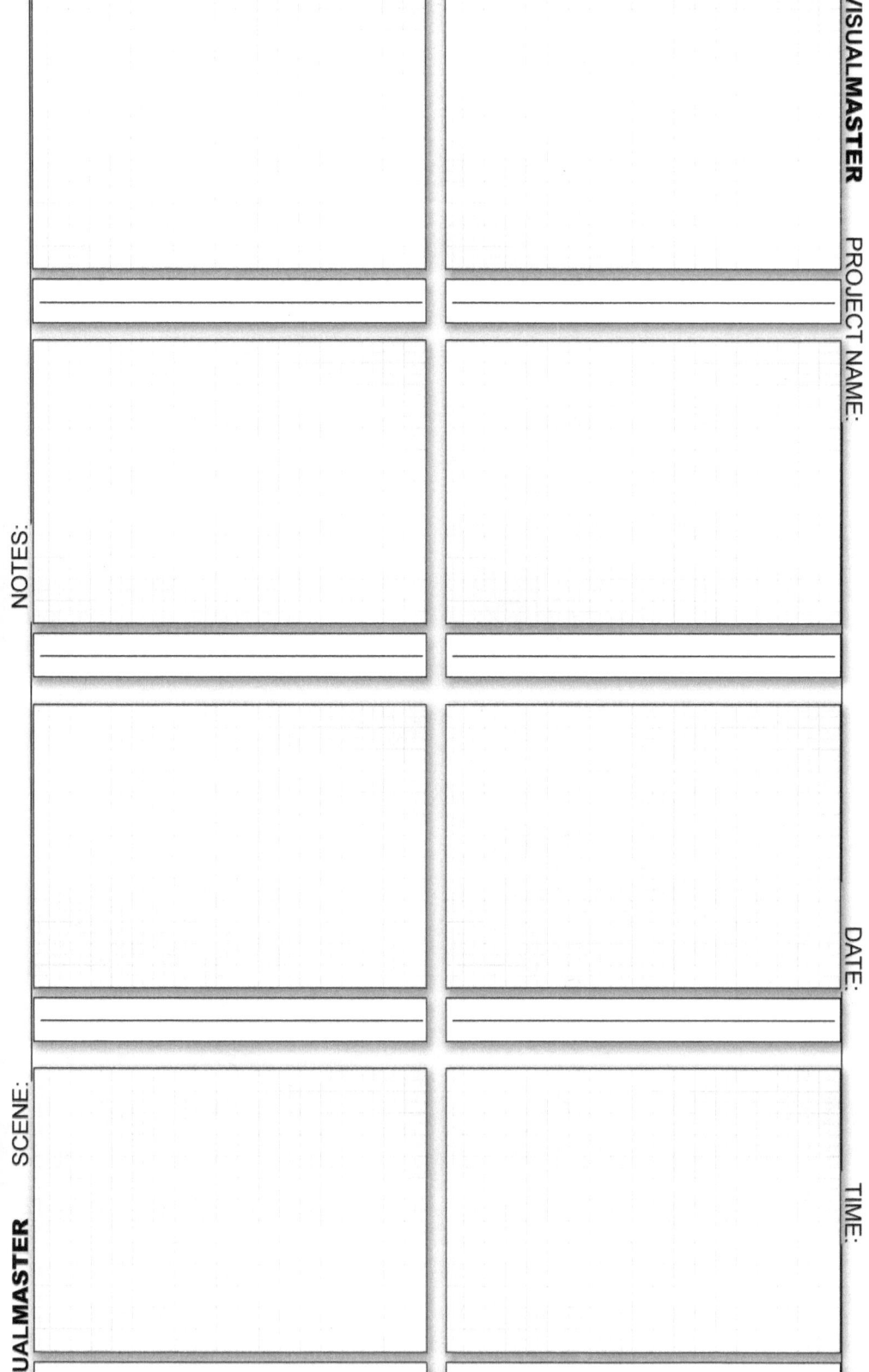

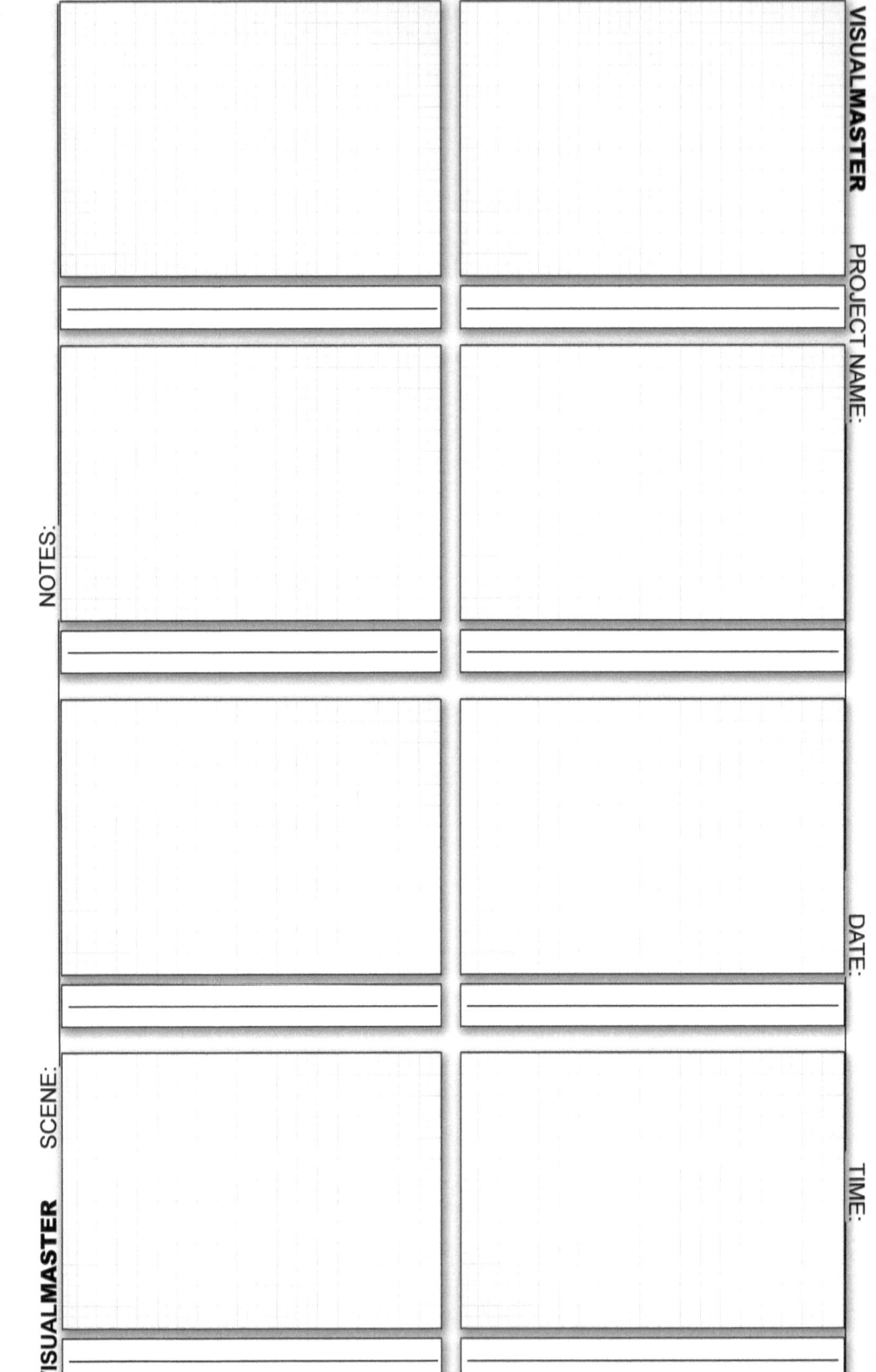

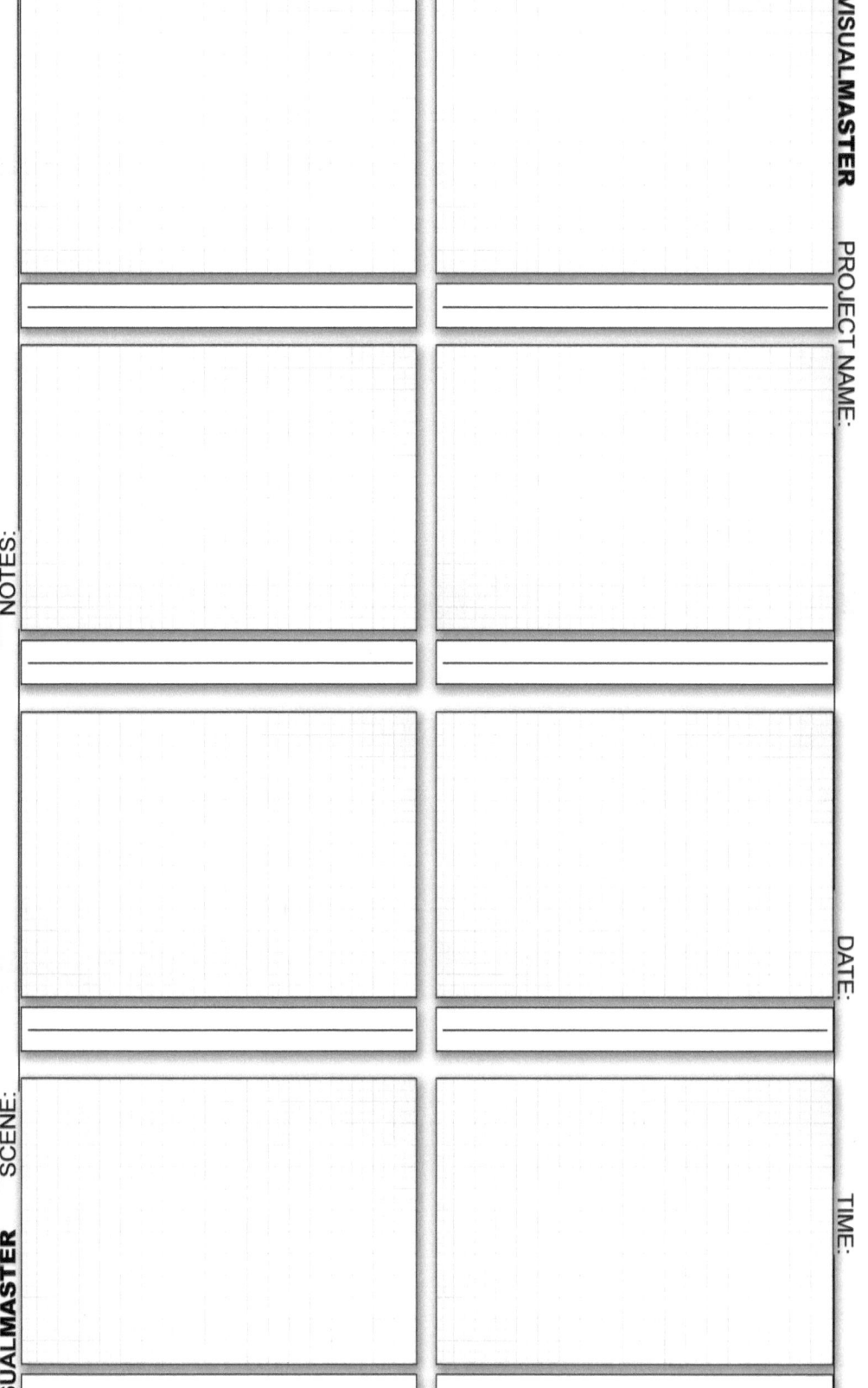

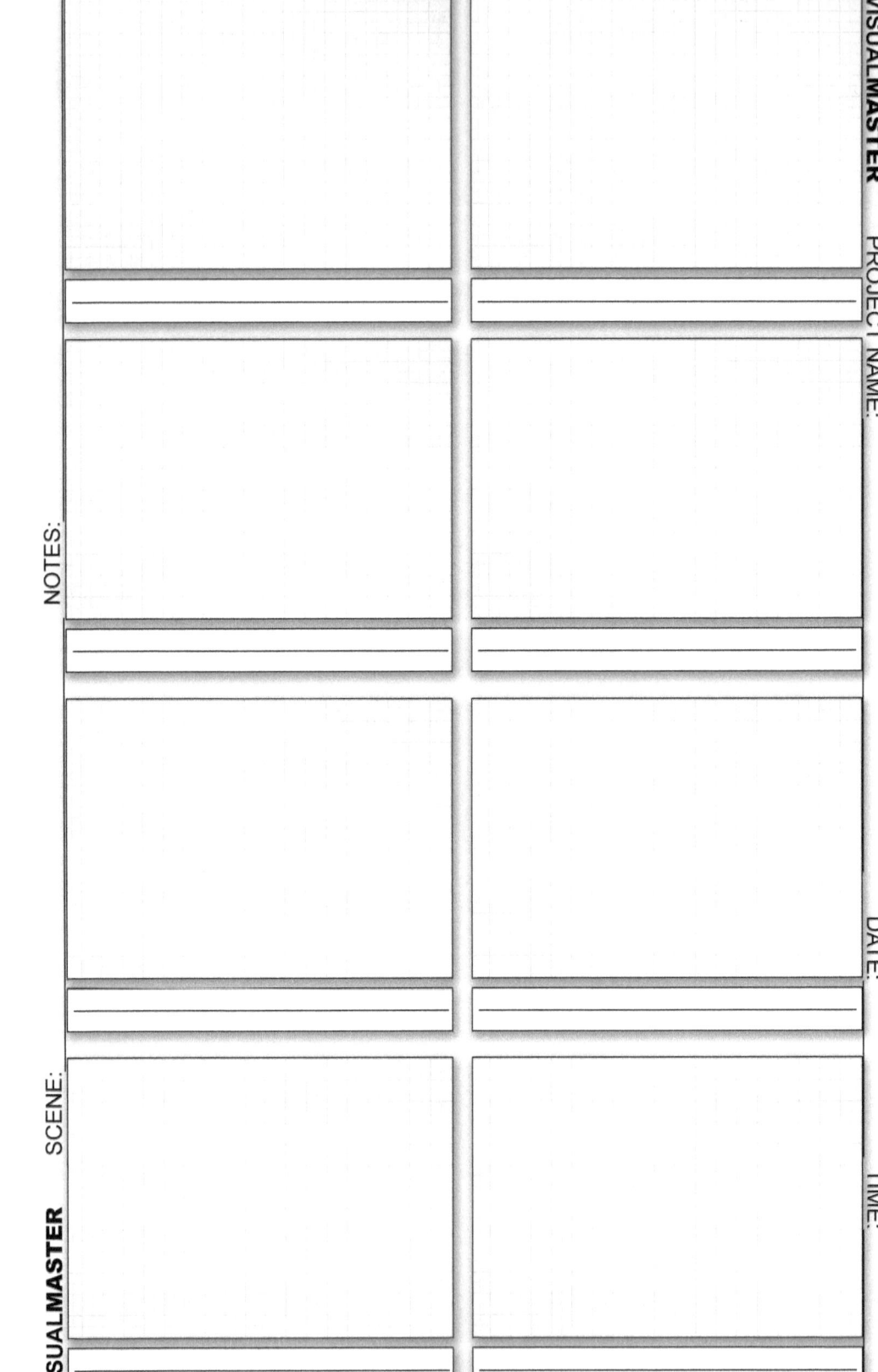

VISUALMASTER

PROJECT NAME:

NOTES:

DATE:

SCENE:

VISUALMASTER

TIME:

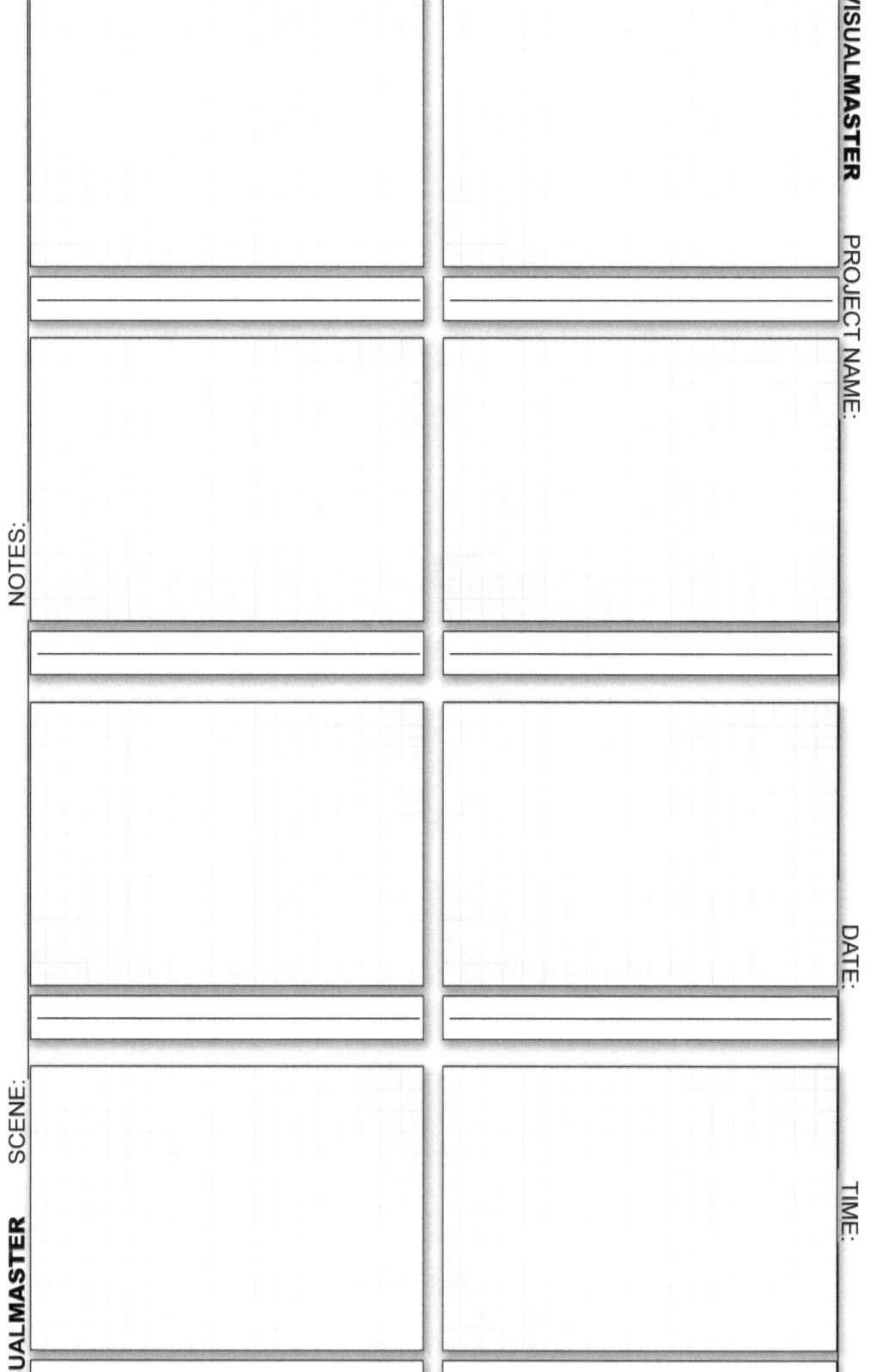

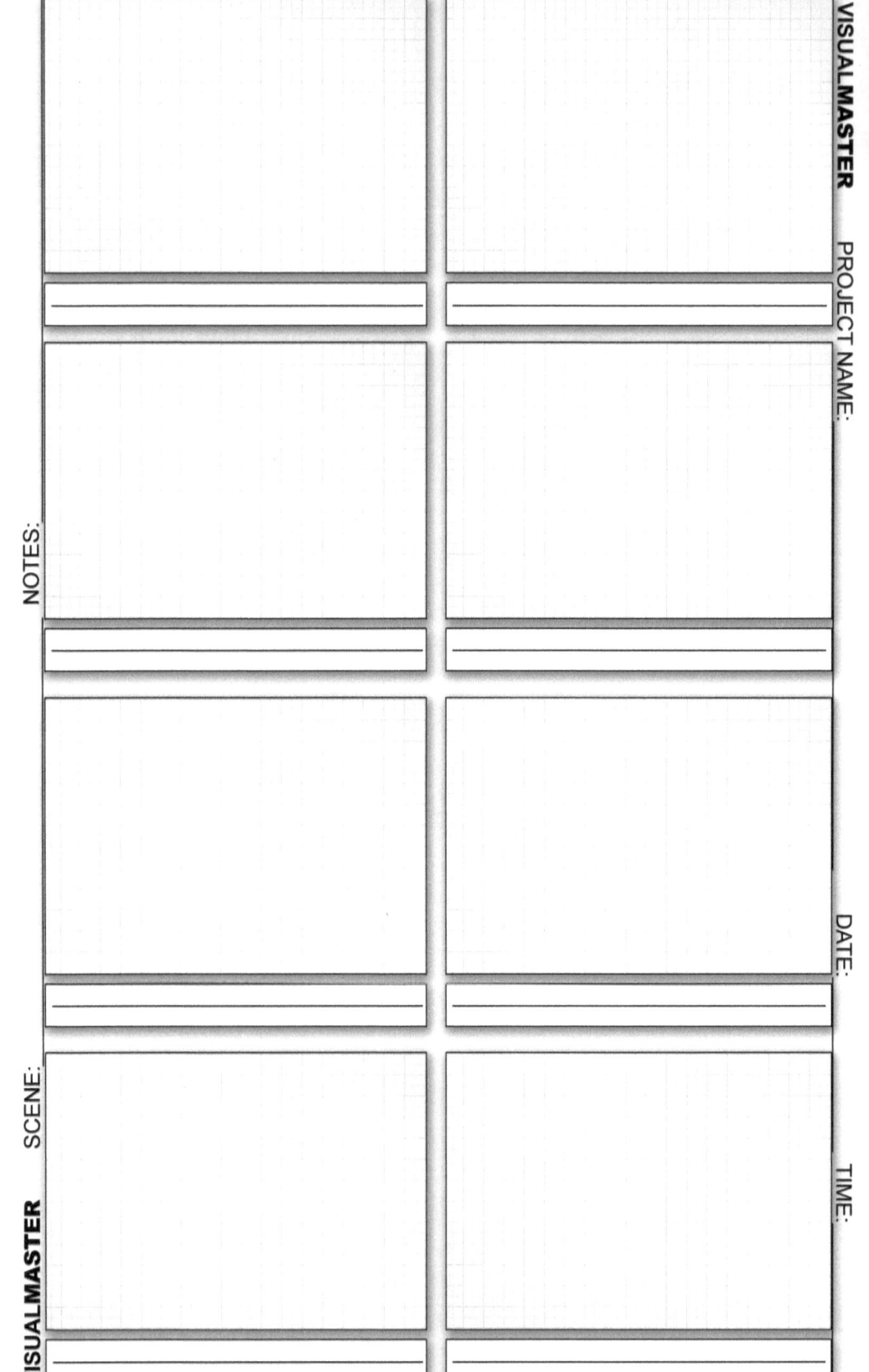

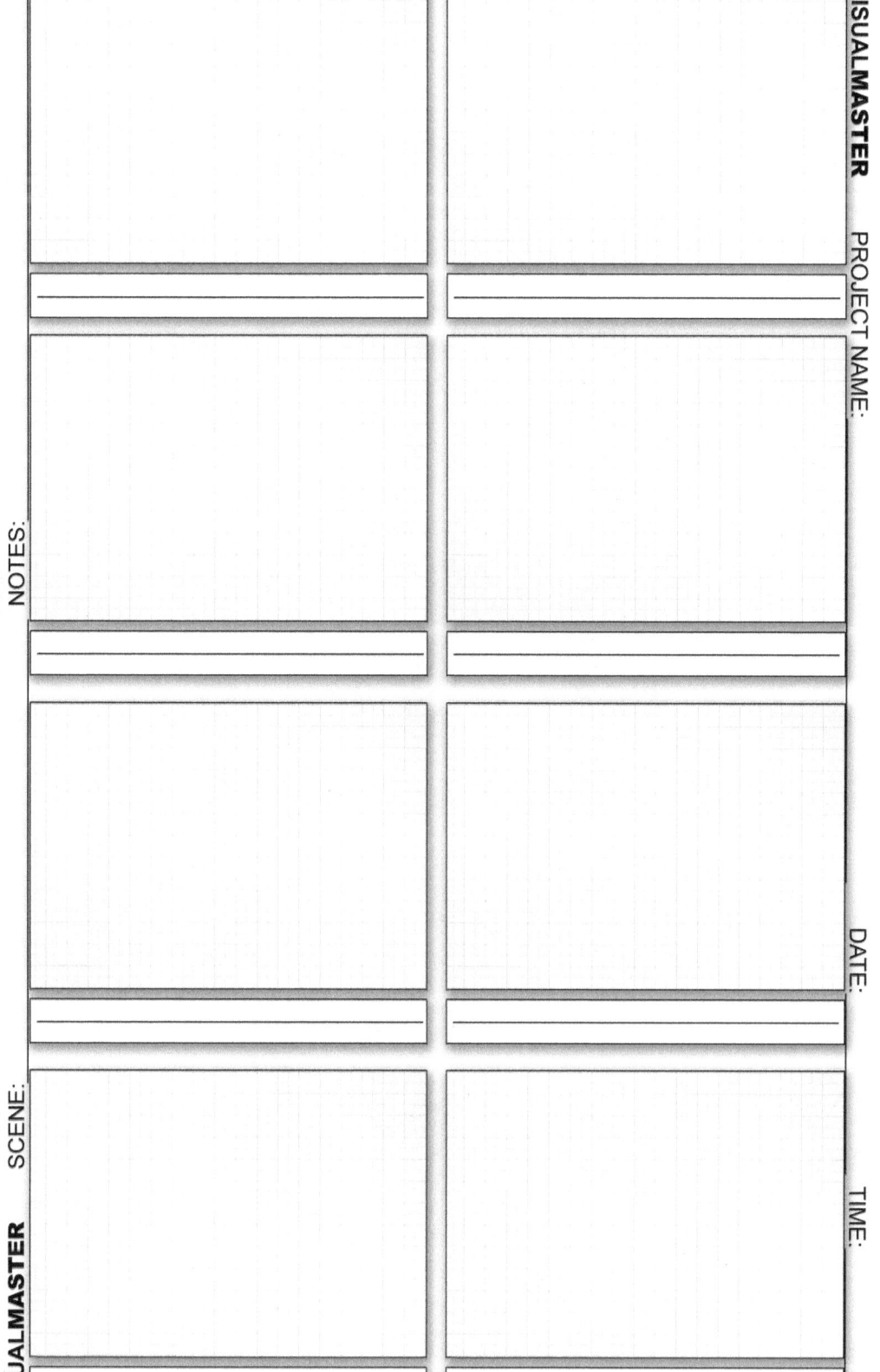

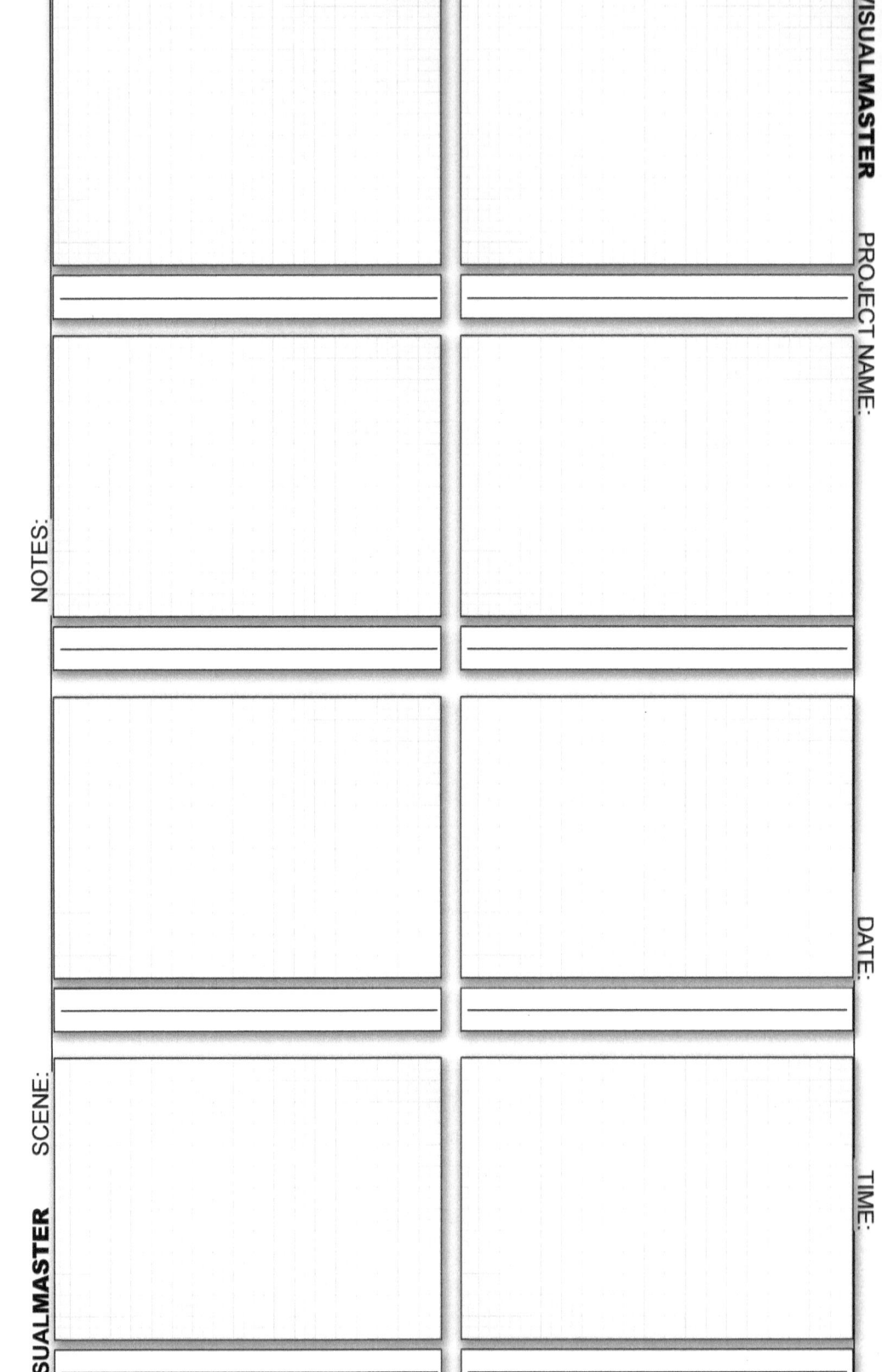

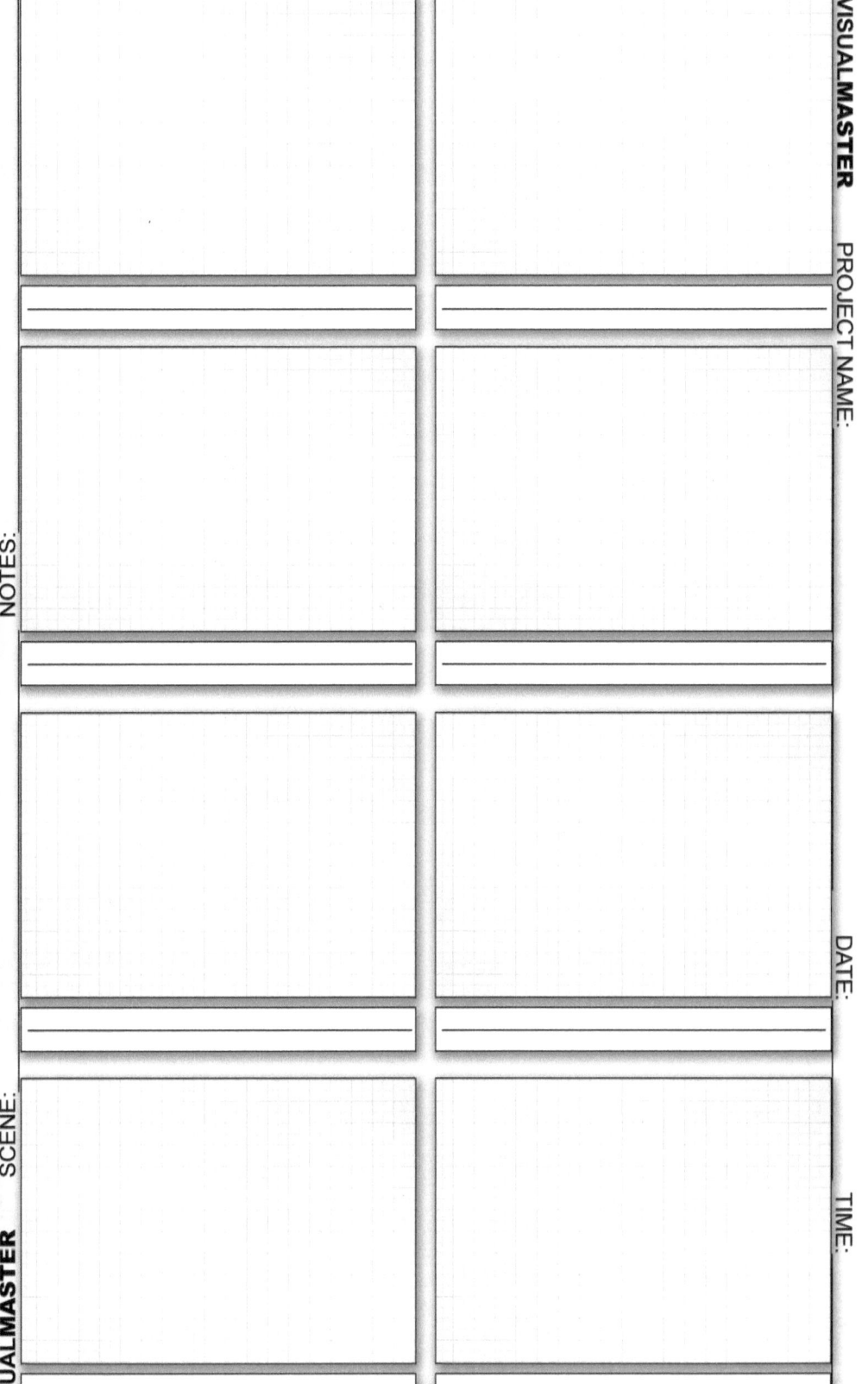

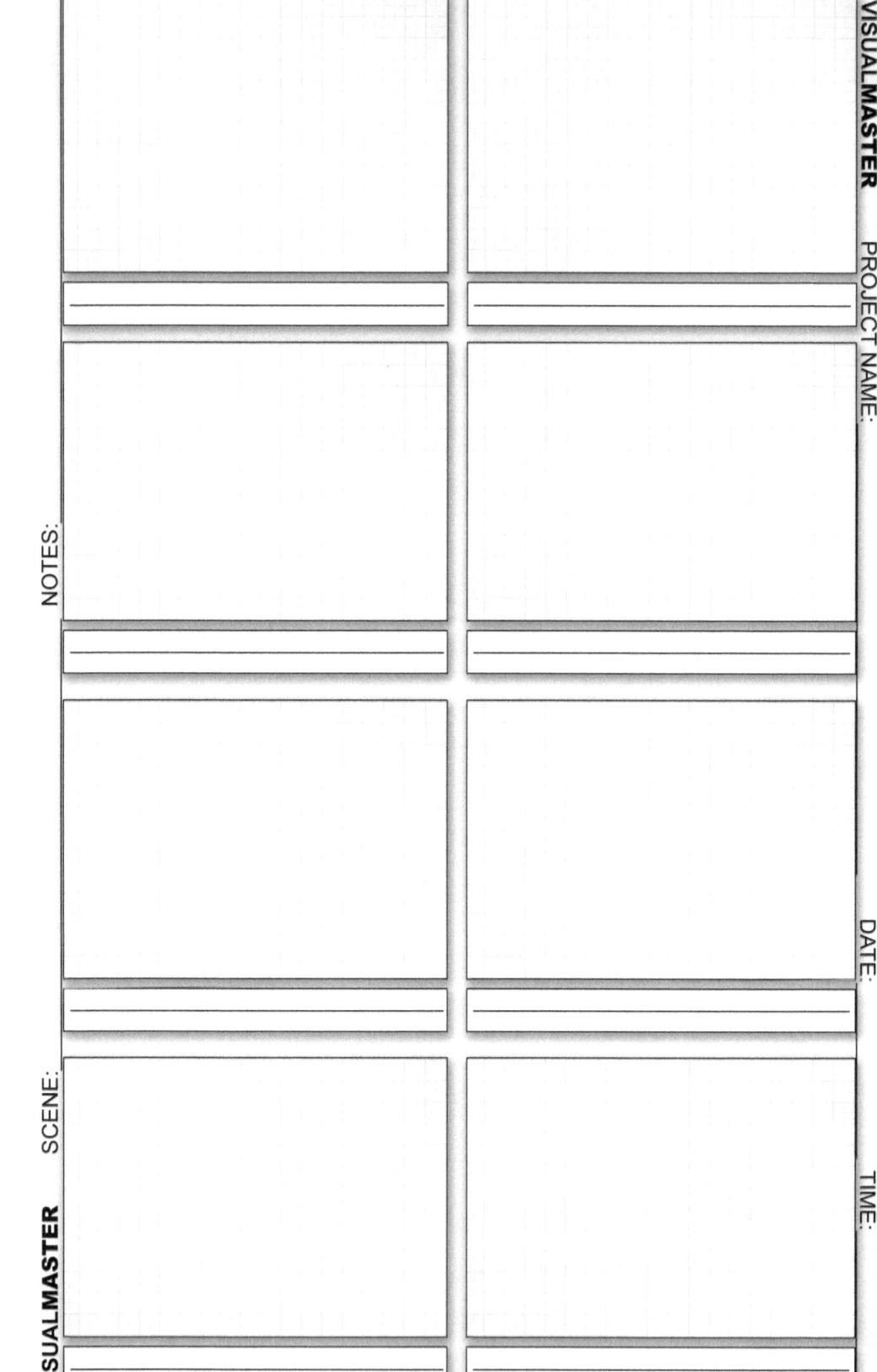

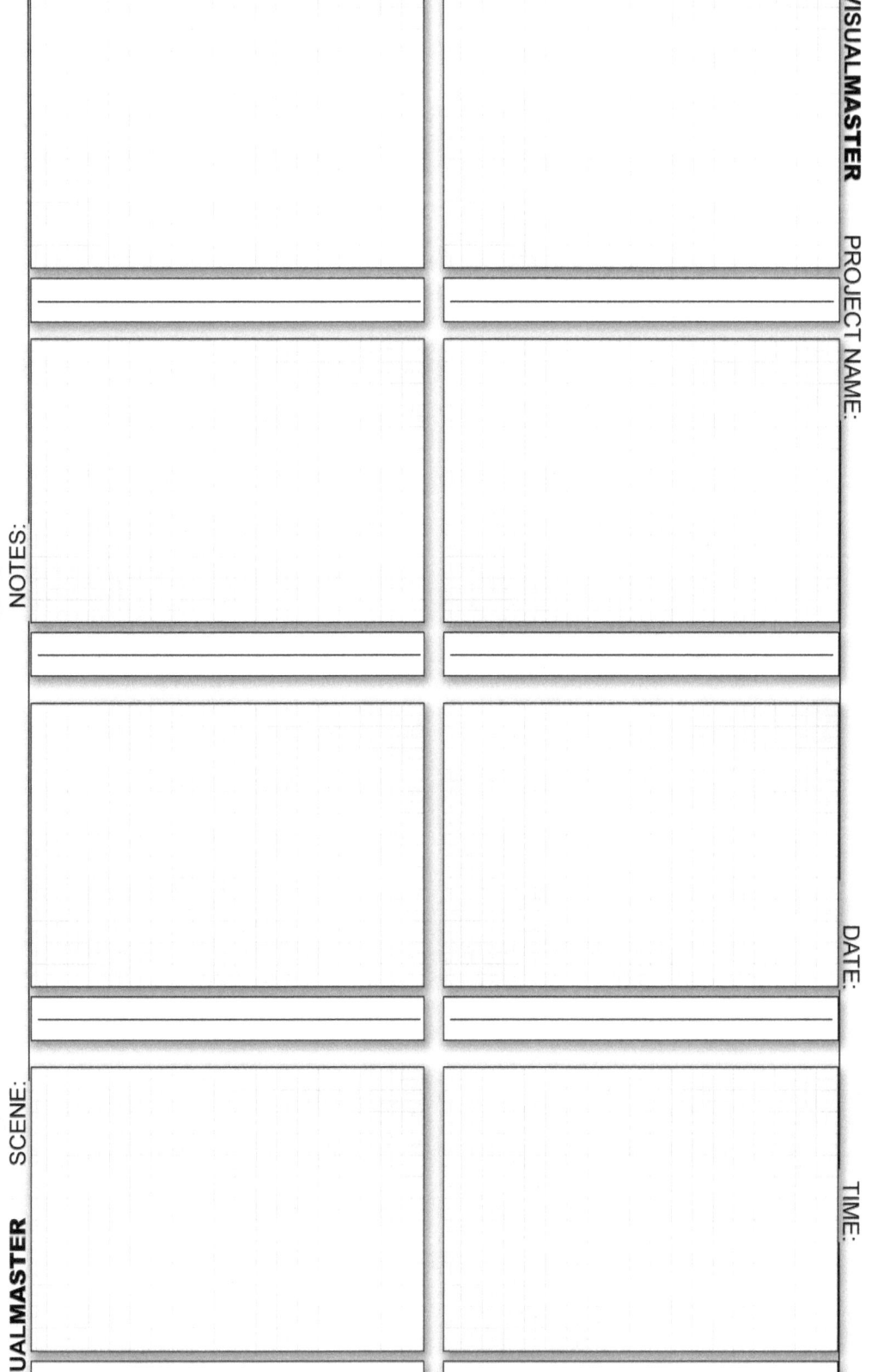

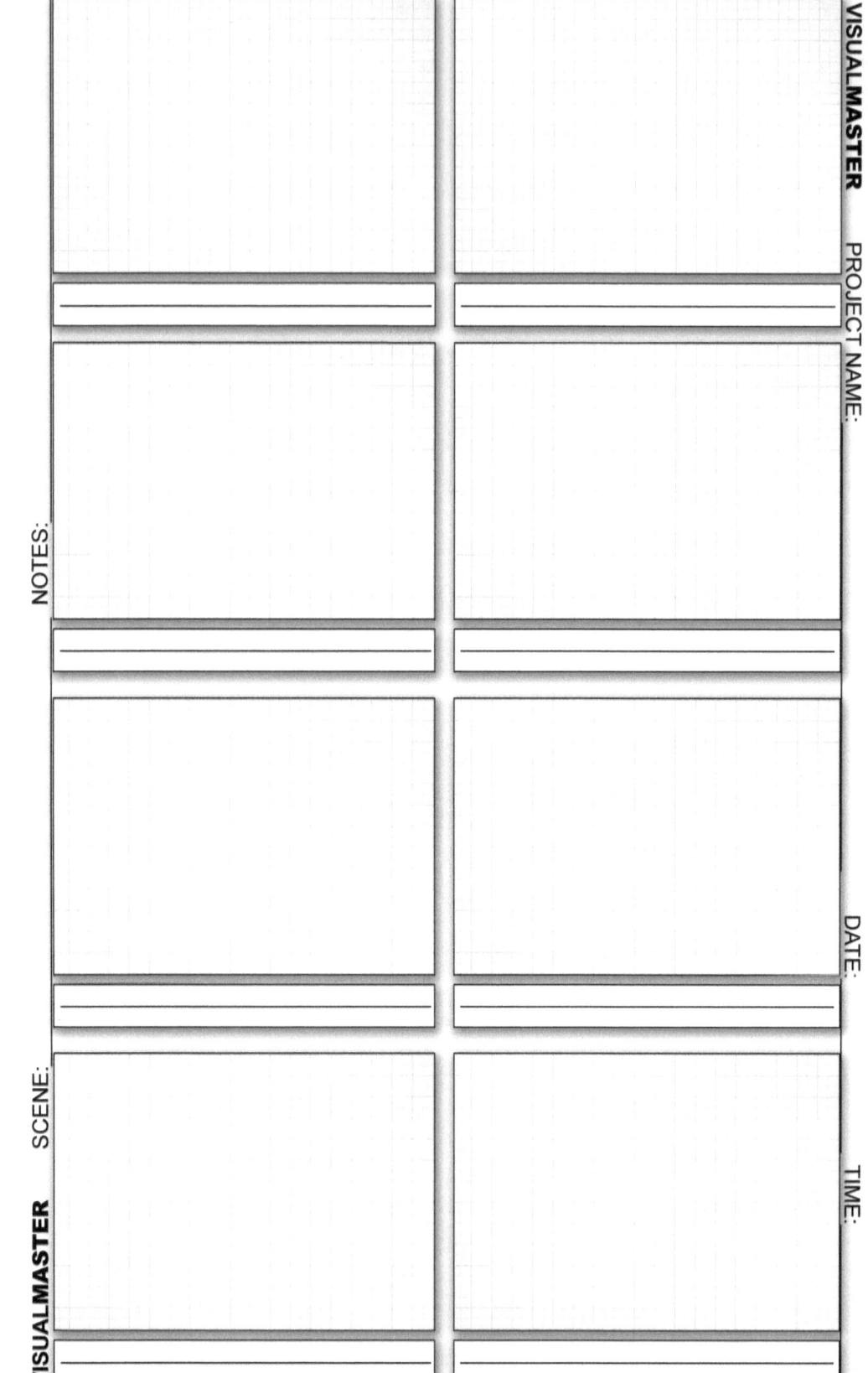

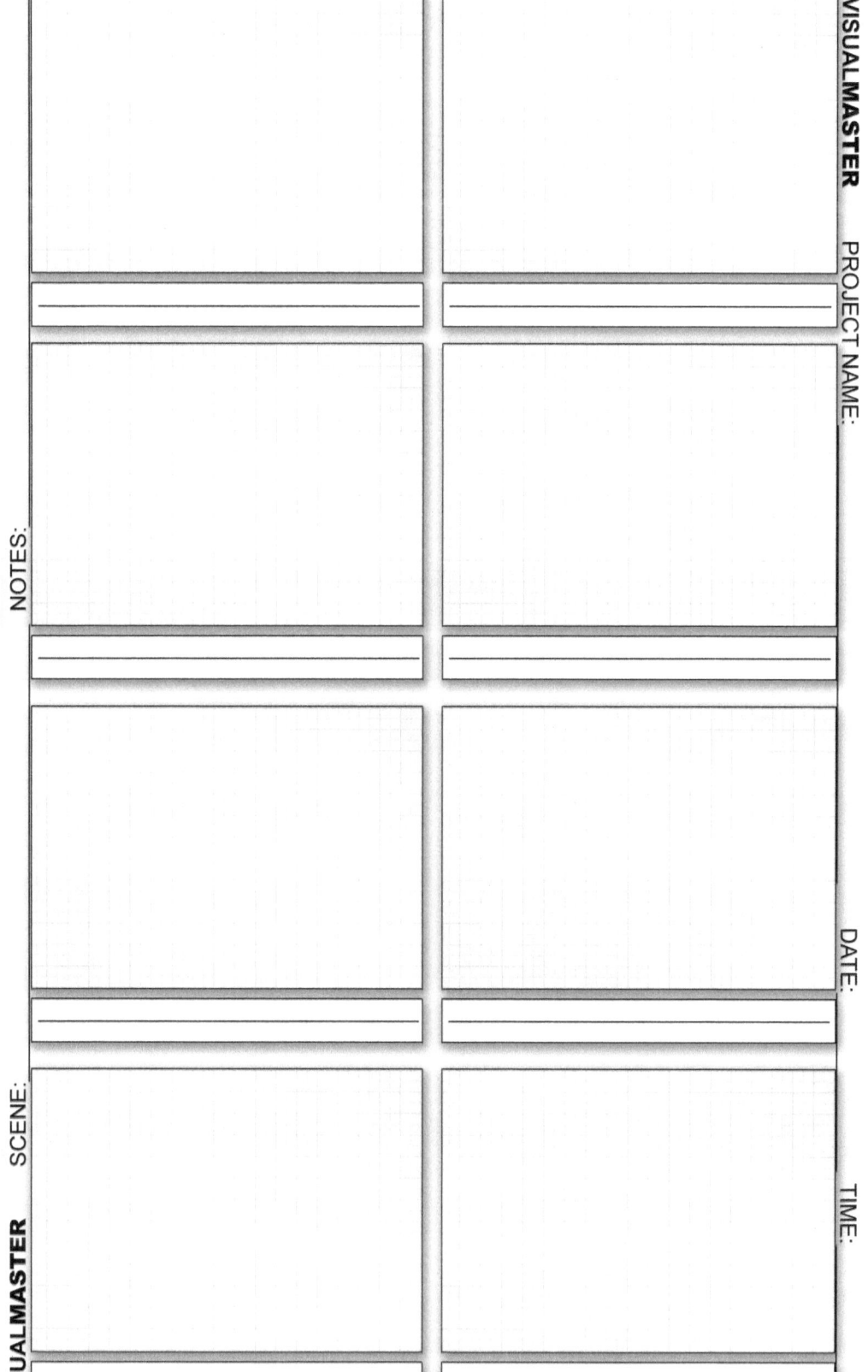

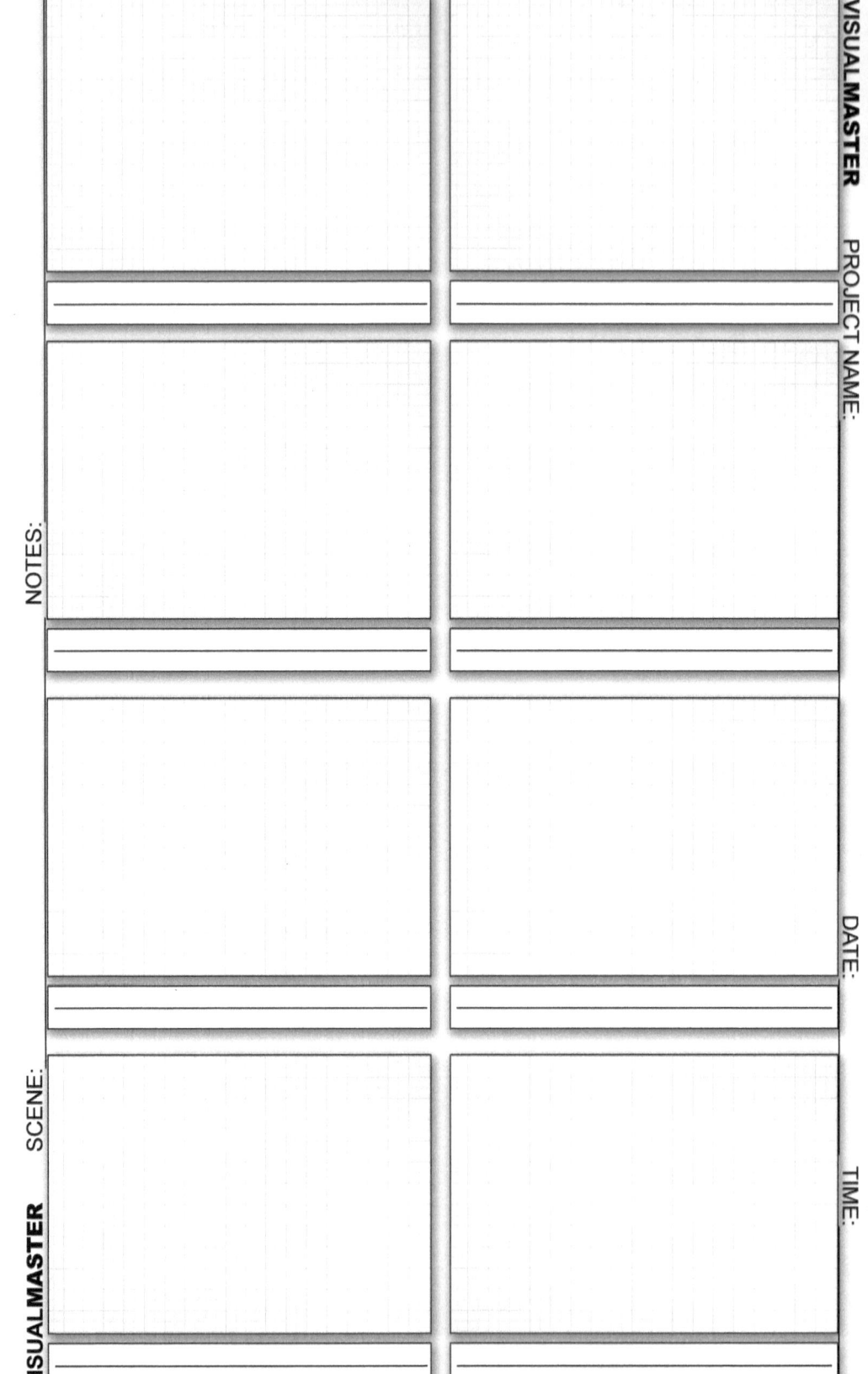

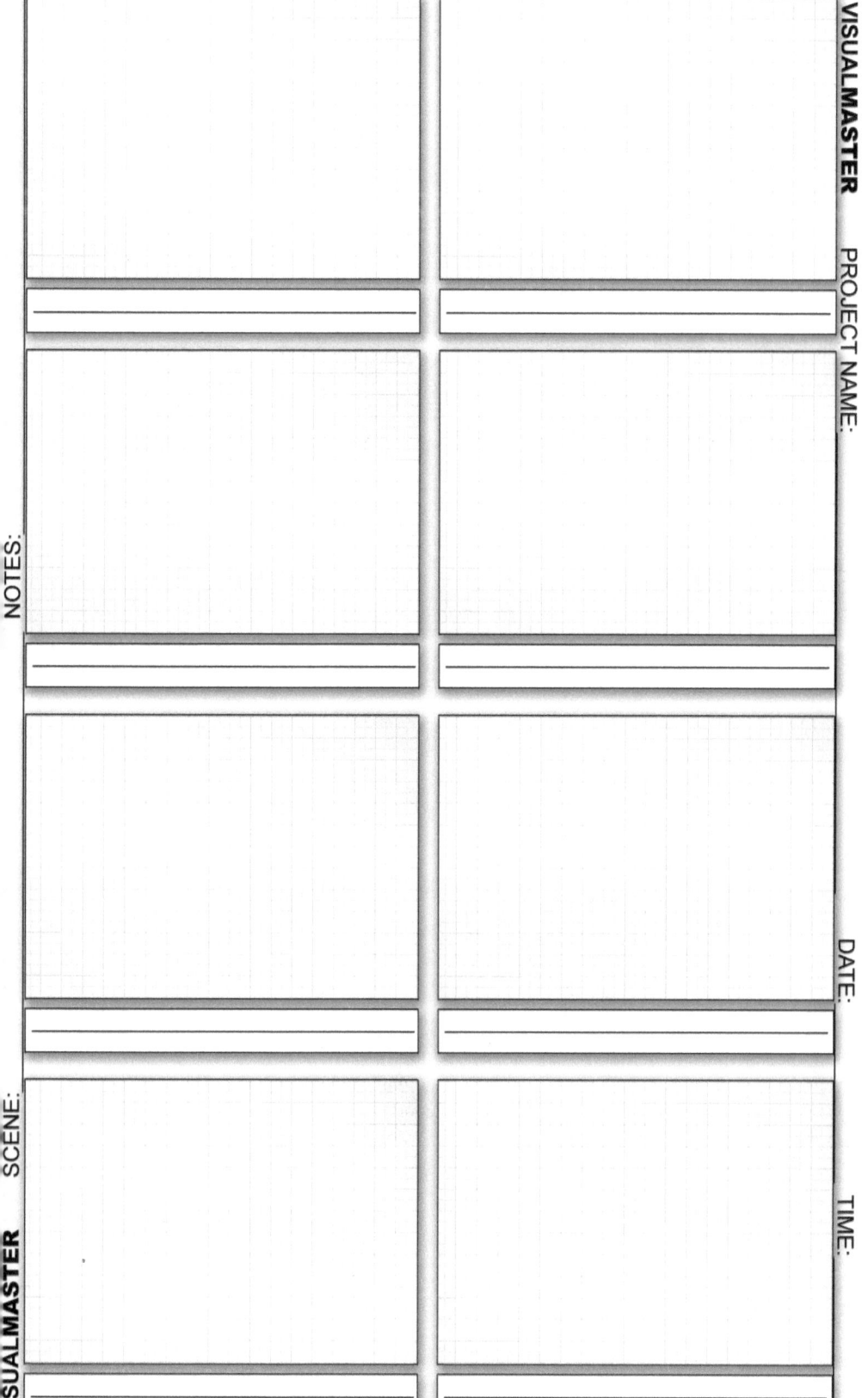

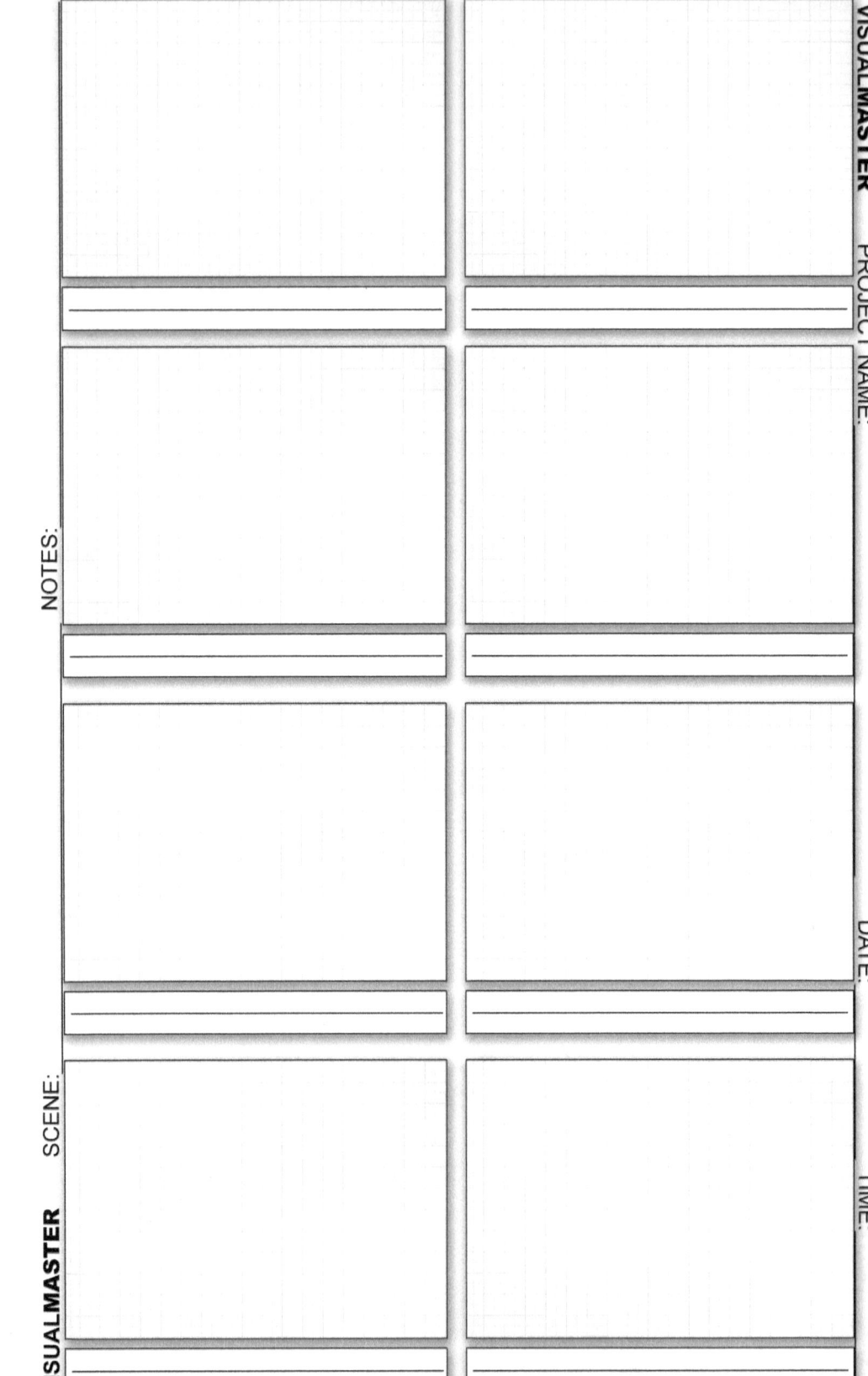

VISUALMASTER   PROJECT NAME: DATE: TIME:

NOTES:

SCENE:

VISUALMASTER

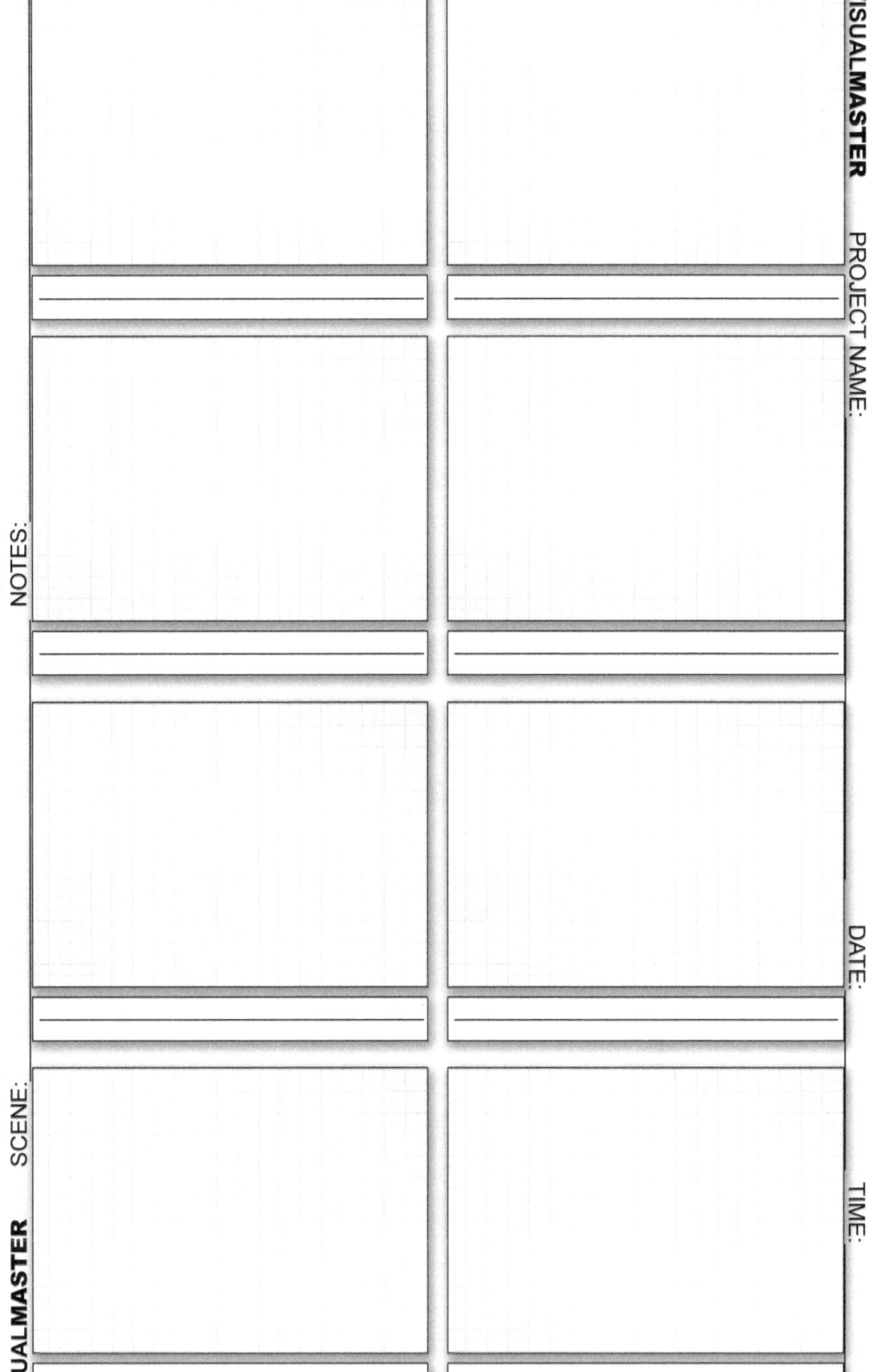

VISUALMASTER   PROJECT NAME: DATE: TIME:

NOTES:

VISUALMASTER   SCENE:

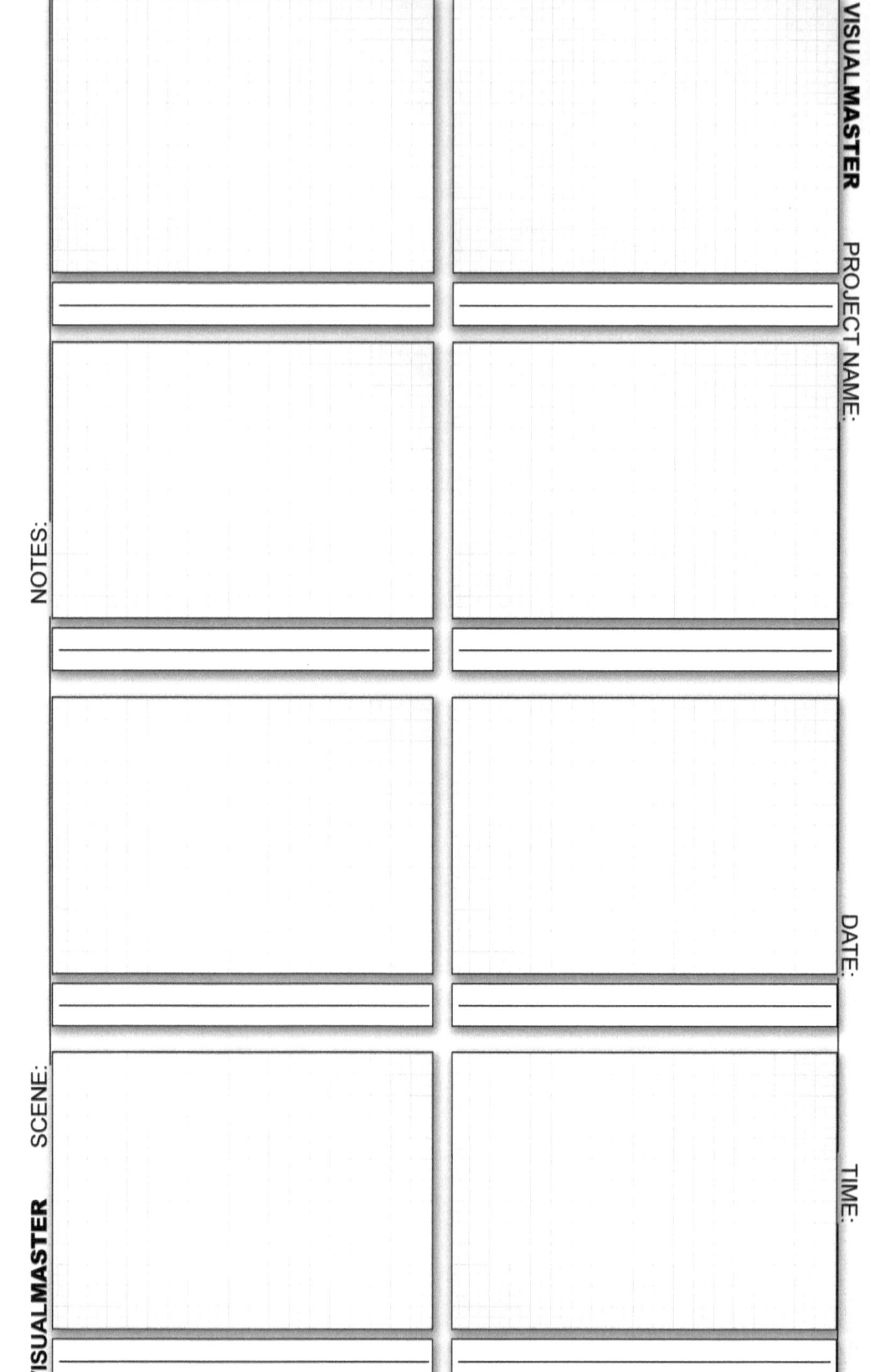

More amazing Journals can be found at:

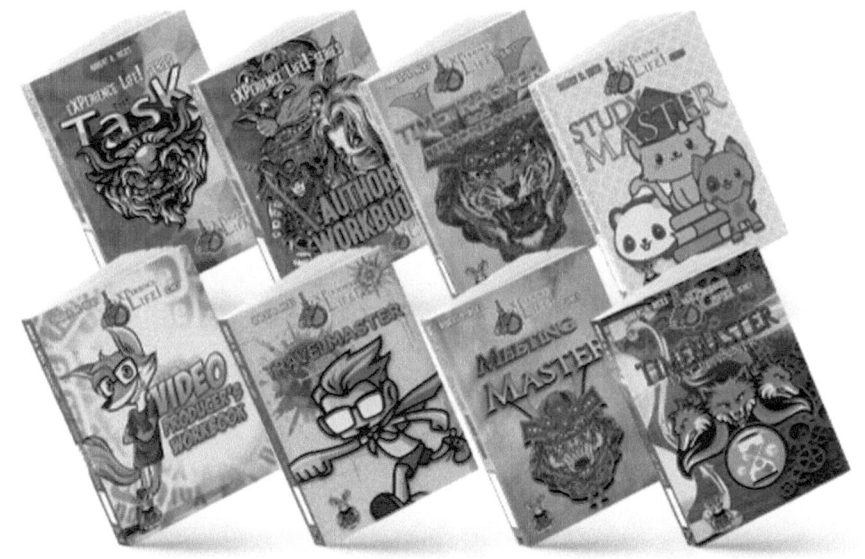

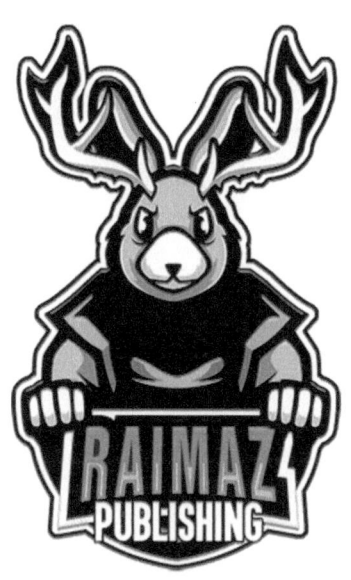

http://www.RAIMAZPUBLISHING.com

www.ingramcontent.com/pod-product-compliance
Lightning Source LLC
Chambersburg PA
CBHW021045180526
45163CB00005B/2293